After honing his culinary skills in his native Lombardy, and working in a number of Michelin-starred restaurants in France and Italy, chef **Alessandro Pavoni** settled in Australia in 2003, landing the role of Executive Chef at Sydney's Park Hyatt. In 2009, he realised his dream of opening his own restaurant and Ormeggio at The Spit was born. Ormeggio was included in *The Australian*'s prestigious Top 50 Restaurants, and has held two coveted Chef's Hats in *The Sydney Morning Herald Good Food Guide* since 2013. In 2014, Alessandro opened Via Alta restaurant in Sydney's Willoughby, featuring the flavours and time-honoured recipes of his beloved Lombardy – and this is the food he shares with us in his first cookbook. His most recent venture, Chiosco by Ormeggio, an Italian street food-inspired kiosk offering breakfast, lunch and dinner, opened in the marina adjacent to Ormeggio in late 2014.

Roberta Muir manages one of Australia's leading cooking schools, Sydney Seafood School at Sydney Fish Market. She holds a Master of Arts degree in Gastronomy from the University of Adelaide, and is the author of the *Sydney Seafood School Cookbook* and *500 Cheeses*; she is co-author of *A Sardinian Cookbook* with Giovanni Pilu and also assisted Janni Kyritsis with his cookbook *Wild Weed Pie*.

To my daughter, Jada Elizabeth Pavoni, who was
but a dream when we started writing this book, and
became a reality by the end … the best reality in the
world. And to my wife, Anna, for enabling me to realise
my dreams, supporting me, being patient and
for loving me. I love you both forever.
ALESSANDRO PAVONI

Franz Scheurer, my best friend and husband, this one's
for you – it always was. You are the one that grounds me
and enables me to do all that I do. Isle of Ewe.
ROBERTA MUIR

A
LOMBARDIAN
COOKBOOK

From the Alps to the lakes of Northern Italy

ALESSANDRO PAVONI & ROBERTA MUIR

Photography by Chris Chen

LANTERN

an imprint of
PENGUIN BOOKS

INTRODUCTION

Growing up in a small village in the Northern Italian province of Lombardy, I was surrounded by a tight-knit extended family. Our daily lives were punctuated by food – hunting, harvesting and foraging for it, preparing it, then sitting down at a table to eat together twice every day. And it wasn't just like this for my family, it was the same for the whole village – our daily lives revolved around food.

Each weekday, after a quick breakfast of milky coffee accompanied by something sweet, usually a biscuit or piece of bread, my brother and I went off to school and *Papà* went to work. At noon, the schools, factories, shops and other workplaces would all down tools and we went home to share a two- or three-course meal. Every lunch time, it was the same – we often started with a pasta *primi* (entrée), such as *Casoncelli alla Bresciana* (Brescian Ravioli with Burnt Butter and Sage, see page 102). In Italy, it's normal to start a meal with just a small bite of pasta. In fact, when I first came to Australia, I was surprised how the amount of pasta served for one would serve a few people back home; when my father first visited he just couldn't understand Australian main-sized pasta serves. The *primi* was followed by a main course (*secondi*) – usually a piece of meat or fish, always served with a few side dishes, as *Papà* loves these at every meal. Sometimes we'd start off with just one antipasto, as is the traditional way – not a large selection, as seems to be the way in Australia. Other times we'd finish with dessert. As a schoolboy, Thursday lunch was my favourite. Without fail, *Mamma* cooked Risotto Milanese (see page 60), with a big, juicy *Cotoletta Milanese* (Crumbed Veal Cutlets Milan-style, see page 168) alongside, and I remember looking forward to this feast all week.

Then it was back to school or work at 2:30 p.m. When *Papà* finished work at 6 p.m., we'd all sit down for our evening meal, which, like lunch, was always two or three courses. Polenta often appeared on our dinner table. The first day it was the soft polenta on page 49, which *Mamma* stirred in a copper pot over the fire, then the next day she grilled the leftovers (see page 54), as no food was ever wasted. Families eating their meals together was a cultural tradition, and I want to continue this with my daughter, Jada, as she grows up.

The food we ate came from what was produced by the surrounding land and lakes. Lombardy is a land-locked region, not much greater than the area of Wales in the UK (or the combined Greater Sydney and Blue Mountains regions in Australia). However, although it is such a small landscape the flavours vary dramatically. Renowned for its combination of Italian Alps, beautiful lakes and fertile plains, Lombardy is Italy's primary livestock and dairy-producing region. Naturally we eat a lot of meat and cheese, as well as freshwater fish from the lakes and risotto rice from the Po Valley. Lake Iseo in the lake district was a 10-minute drive over a mountain from my village, which is in a valley near Franciacorta in the province of Brescia. Even in this short distance, the ingredients, flavours and dishes differed due to the change in climate and produce available. In fact, the lake district has a micro-climate that is more thought of as Mediterranean, perfect for growing grapes, olives and citrus much further north than is generally expected. So Lombardy boasts not only the rustic, hearty, wintry meat and dairy-based fare associated with the Alps, but also the lighter, more summery olive oil and fish-based specialities of the lakes.

Family is central to life in Lombardy, and this basically determined where we went and how we spent our leisure time. We never ventured all that far from home when I was a child. I didn't visit the capital, Milan, until I was an adult, although my grandparents went there for their honeymoon, as was common at the time, and I remember hearing their stories as it was the biggest trip of their lives. I loved the countryside and the freedom it brought and disliked the whole idea of cities.

One of my cousins married someone from the Lombardian plains around Mantua, and once or twice a month my family drove 45 minutes to visit them for lunch. I enjoyed these trips, not least because it was a chance to eat different regional specialties; there's a huge emphasis on vegetables and the pasta is different there, too. In winter, the plains are foggy and therefore much more humid, making them ideal for growing the sweetest pumpkins you could ever taste, which they use to fill the pumpkin and amaretti ravioli on page 105 that Mantua is known for. This micro-climate also creates different-tasting salumi, such as prosciutto and salami – even to a child, they were noticeably softer and more tender.

On the weekends and during the school holidays we visited my grandmother's house high in the mountains, 1000 metres above sea level. It was the last village at the end of the road – if you wanted to go further up the mountain you'd have to hike or ride a mountain bike. When we arrived we'd park our car and not use it til weeks later when it was time to drive home. We kids spent our days exploring waterfalls and rock climbing right outside the doorstep – it was like an outdoor gym. There was nothing to fear in nature and every day was an adventure. As I grew older, I got into snowboarding, ice climbing, free climbing and even helicopter snowboarding. I've always loved an adrenaline rush!

Only 60 people lived in my *Nonna*'s village permanently, although the population swelled to 2000 during August, Italy's summer holiday month. During our time there, we only ate the food from the local area, which boasted a bounty of chicken, sheep, mountain goats, game, fresh milk and local butter. Plus, the mountain air is perfect for curing the meats such as bresaola (see page 6) and cheeses, including the gorgonzola, Grana Padano, taleggio and stracchino that Lombardy is famed for, so we always ate well. There was one shop that stuck to basics like salt, flour and sugar, and sold freshly baked bread each day, but the rest of our food was hunted, grown or foraged. There was only one bar/restaurant in town (an extension of the one shop!), serving hunters' food, especially the spit-roasted meat, *spiedo alla Bresciana*, on page 108, that is Brescia's speciality.

My grandfather married *Nonna* when she was young. He had eight brothers and, as their mother had died young, it became *Nonna*'s role to look after and cook for all of them and their wives and children, feeding them three meals each day. She spent a lot of her time cooking and I loved helping her, standing by her side and asking her questions. I even wanted to learn the dirty jobs, like gutting and plucking chickens and cleaning frogs, as well as preparing the game that my *Nonno*, an accomplished hunter, caught.

For me, these were convivial times as I helped *Nonna* cook Sunday lunch every week for 16 to 20 people, starting at 6 a.m. I have such clear and happy memories of being part of an amazing family, and at *Nonna*'s side I learnt firsthand the power of food to nourish and bring joy. This is what led me to become a chef, as I wanted to give this feeling to others – it's an emotion you can't buy.

After having spent the first two decades of my life without leaving Lombardy, apart from our annual family holiday to the seaside in Liguria, where the seafood was a revelation, my adventurous spirit and curiosity finally got the better of me. I'd been working in restaurant kitchens since I was 15, and I now took on stints in Michelin-starred restaurants in France and Northern Italy.

The great thing about being a chef is that you can earn a living anywhere. On a whim I bought a ticket to Australia, thinking I could always go back home if it didn't work out. After following the usual backpacking trail around Australia, and meeting my future wife, Anna, I took off for Bermuda. There was a lot going on in my life at that time and I really wanted a change – change of scenery, change of language, change of life. I also wished to learn English, but having come from an alpine region of Italy, I wanted to experience a warmer climate and felt that England would be too cold. So in 2003, I came back to Anna and Sydney, where I have lived ever since and put down roots. After initially arriving speaking barely a word of English, I soon found a home away from home in Leichhardt, Sydney's 'Little Italy'. This didn't exactly further my ambition to speak English as I could get away with just speaking Italian. However, my English improved dramatically thanks to Anna!

Cheffing also gives me the adrenaline rush I love getting from extreme sports (although these days longboarding and riding my Harley Davidson are more my pace). I'd conquered a number of health scares since my late teens; I was diagnosed with the first of three cancers when I was just 19. Life in Sydney was cruising along and I was really enjoying my time as Executive Chef for the Park Hyatt, then, when I was 37, I had my first heart attack – during a yoga class, would you believe it? Like my initial bone cancer diagnosis, this led me to assess my life and what I wanted to achieve. I decided to go out on a limb and, in 2009, opened my first restaurant, Ormeggio at The Spit – it was a dream come true! I love being my own boss, even though it's a huge responsibility, and it has been wonderful creating this contemporary Italian restaurant, combining my love of Italian flavours with both new and traditional techniques. In 2014, I returned to my Lombardian roots, opening Via Alta in Sydney's Willoughby to showcase the food of my childhood.

I have such beautiful memories of my early days in Lombardy. The lessons I learned about family, food and tradition, and how intertwined they are, are at the heart of everything I do today. Even now, thousands of kilometres and a hemisphere away from Lombardy, it's the traditions and food culture of my childhood that anchors me to the past and present and inspires my future.

For me, this book is a taste of Lombardy, and home. I hope it not only introduces you to the unique food of this diverse region, but keeps it alive by inspiring you to cook my recipes and enjoy these flavours in your own home. So when you sit down to a table of Lombardian dishes with your loved ones, as I did twice every day during my childhood, these traditions will continue, transplanted to a new home.

ANTI PASTI

I grew up eating four-course meals, which is the traditional Italian way: *antipasto*, *primo*, *secondo* and *dolce*. At home, our antipasto (literally 'before the meal') is just one dish served as an entrée, not the mixture of dishes Aussies often expect when they think of antipasto (that's *antipasti misti*). Following this tradition, the recipes in this chapter are entrée-sized, although some, like the vitello tonnato on page 14, I often make in larger quantities for celebrations, and others, such as the beef meatballs on page 20, are perfect finger food for parties.

BRESAOLA CON RUCOLA E GRANA
BRESAOLA WITH ROCKET AND PARMESAN

Serves 6

1 large handful baby rocket leaves
extra virgin olive oil, for drizzling
salt flakes and freshly ground
    black pepper
300 g sliced bresaola
    (see page 225)
200 g Grana Padano, shaved
Chisolini (see below), to serve

The cool, dry air of the Alps is perfect for air-drying beef. When I was 19 I had a job with our local butcher, who taught me his method for making bresaola, based on his grandfather's 100-year-old recipe. These days the beef is only salted and lightly smoked, but his grandfather first marinated it in red wine, so the acidity helped break down the meat and tenderised it.

Place the rocket in bowl and toss with a drizzle of oil, a pinch of salt and a good grind of pepper.

Arrange the bresaola slices in a single layer on a platter, then top with the rocket and Grana and another grind of pepper. Serve with *chisolini*.

CHISOLINI
FRIED PASTRIES TO SERVE WITH SALUMI

Makes about 35

1 teaspoon dried yeast
½ teaspoon caster sugar
150 ml lukewarm water
1⅔ cups (250 g) 00 flour
    (see page 225), plus extra
    for dusting
2 teaspoons fine salt
grapeseed oil, for deep-frying

These fried pastries are always served with bresaola and other salumi. In Lombardy we use lard; you can too if you like. A pasta machine is very handy for rolling the dough thinly enough.

Combine the yeast, sugar and 100 ml of the water in a bowl and stir to dissolve the yeast. Set aside for a few minutes until the mixture just begins to bubble.

Sift the flour and salt into a bowl and make a well in the centre. Pour the yeast mixture and remaining water into the well and, using two fingers, gradually mix the flour from the side of the well into the water until it is all incorporated and the dough just comes together.

Tip out onto a clean, dry, lightly floured workbench and knead with the heels of your hands to form a smooth dough. Place in a flour-dusted bowl, cover with a clean tea towel and set aside in a warm place for 1 hour or until slightly risen.

Roll out the dough on a lightly floured workbench to a thickness of 3 mm. Using a round 6.5 cm pastry cutter, cut into rounds and leave for 10 minutes or until slightly risen.

Heat oil for deep-frying in a heavy-based saucepan or deep-fryer and, working in batches, fry the dough discs for 1½ minutes, then turn and fry for another 1½ minutes or until they are puffed and golden. Drain on paper towel.

Serve with bresaola or other salumi.

NSALATA DI GAMBERI DI FIUME E ASPARAGI

YABBY AND ASPARAGUS SALAD

We have a little creek in the valley near my home. The water's very clear and we swim in it during the day – but in the middle of the night everyone goes there to catch yabbies. I'm not sure if that's when the yabbies come out or if it's because it's illegal! We go with our friends, then we take the yabbies back to someone's home and make spaghetti with them, or this salad. I remember yabbying with my uncles and cousins, then when we returned, our mums would cook them for us – it was such a treat to have a meal simply consisting of yabbies. You can add cherry tomatoes and shaved raw artichokes to make a more substantial dish, if you like.

Serves 6

12 live yabbies (see page 227)

12 spears green asparagus, peeled, bases trimmed

12 spears white asparagus, peeled, bases trimmed

salt flakes

1 handful (about ½ cup) flat-leaf parsley leaves, finely chopped

Dressing

salt flakes

½ teaspoon caster sugar

2 tablespoons strained lemon juice

1 teaspoon Dijon mustard

2 tablespoons extra virgin olive oil

Place the yabbies in a deep bowl and wrap tightly in a towel. Place in the freezer for 1 hour.

Blanch the green and white asparagus in a saucepan of boiling salted water for 4 minutes or until just tender, then drain and place in iced water to cool. Drain and pat dry. Cut the tips off the asparagus and slice in half lengthways, then finely dice the stalks and set both aside.

To make the dressing, place salt to taste, the sugar and lemon juice in a screw-top jar and shake to dissolve. Add the mustard and oil and shake well until emulsified. Set aside.

Bring a large saucepan of salted water to a rapid boil. Remove the yabbies from the freezer and place in the pan. Cook covered for 3 minutes or until they turn orange-red and the tails are tightly curled. Drain and place in iced water. (Depending on the size of the saucepan, you may need to cook the yabbies in batches as you want the water to return to the boil as quickly as possible.)

When the yabbies are cool enough to handle, twist off the heads and discard. Using kitchen scissors, cut through the centre of the underside of the tail and gently peel the shell away from the meat. Trim off the end where the flesh joined the head. Halve the bodies lengthways and remove any dark intestine. If the claws are large enough, you can crack them and remove the meat if you like.

Combine the asparagus, yabby meat and parsley in a bowl, then toss with just enough of the dressing to coat well.

Arrange on a platter or individual plates, add a final drizzle of dressing, if desired, and serve.

TARTARA DI TROTA

RAINBOW TROUT TARTARE

This is a very traditional dish – I love it! I learnt to make this when I was 15 and working in my first restaurant on Lake Garda. It can be made with meat or seafood. Traditionally it's brought to the table with all the ingredients separate (like a French steak tartare) and the waiter mixes it there. In Lombardy, I love to eat the meat version at Il Frate in Brescia. Some people make it with chopped Ligurian olives – I don't like them in this but you can suit yourself.

Preheat the oven to 180°C.

Chop the ocean trout finely and set aside.

Place the shallot, capers, cornichon, parsley and chives on a chopping board and chop together until finely minced.

Place the egg yolks in a large bowl, then add the lemon juice and whisk while slowly drizzling in the oil until emulsified. Stir in the shallot mixture, and salt and pepper to taste. Add the ocean trout and stir well to almost form a paste, then set aside.

Place the baguette slices on a baking tray, drizzle with a little extra oil, sprinkle with salt and bake for 15 minutes or until crisp and golden.

Place the trout mixture on a platter, sprinkle with lemon zest, then serve with the baguette slices alongside (or spoon some of the trout mixture onto a few baguette slices).

Serves 6

500 g sashimi-grade ocean trout fillets, skin off, pin-boned

1 golden shallot, finely chopped

1 tablespoon small salted capers, rinsed, dried, finely chopped

3 cornichons, finely chopped

1 handful (about ½ cup) flat-leaf parsley leaves, finely chopped

1 tablespoon finely chopped chives

2 egg yolks

¼ cup (60 ml) strained lemon juice

100 ml extra virgin olive oil, plus extra for drizzling

salt flakes and freshly ground white pepper

1 sourdough baguette, thinly sliced on the diagonal

finely grated zest of 1 lemon

RITTATA DI ERBE AMARE

FRITTATA OF BITTER HERBS

This versatile recipe can be served hot or cold. It's great for breakfast, offered as part of a mixed antipasti, or served as an entrée or light main course. The quantities can be halved if you only have a small frying pan. In Italy we use whatever bitter herbs or wild greens are on hand, often including a spicy bitter herb we call *erba amara* – that may just be the name in my dialect – I think it is part of the mint family. It's not available in Australia so I use regular mint here instead. We use hops and nettles when they're in season and, while they aren't traditional, you could also add rocket or nasturtium leaves.

To make the lemon mascarpone cream, combine the mascarpone and lemon zest, then season with salt. Place in a small serving bowl, cover with plastic film and, if making ahead of time, refrigerate. Remove from the refrigerator 30 minutes before serving.

Bring a large saucepan of salted water to the boil. Add the chicory, dandelion, watercress and mint and return to the boil, then boil for 3 minutes. Drain and place in iced water. When cold, squeeze well to remove any excess liquid. Pat dry, roughly chop and place in a large bowl. Add the eggs and a good pinch of salt, then mix lightly with a fork.

Turn on the oven overhead grill function to high.

Meanwhile, melt the butter in a large ovenproof frying pan over high heat. Add the chives and cook for 1 minute. Add the egg mixture, stir to combine and cook for 2–3 minutes or until set around the edge.

Place the pan under the hot grill and cook for 3–5 minutes or until set in the middle, watching it closely as it can burn quickly. Remove from the oven and slip a spatula or egg lift around the side and under the frittata to loosen it. Place a large plate on top of the frying pan and, using a thick cloth so you don't burn yourself, turn the pan over so the frittata is on the plate. Place a serving plate on top of the frittata and invert it again so the green herbs are on top. Set aside to cool to room temperature.

Serve with the room temperature lemon mascarpone cream in a bowl on the side.

Serves 8

salt flakes

2 bunches chicory, stems discarded

100 g dandelion leaves (available from good greengrocers)

1 large handful (about 1 cup) watercress leaves

1 handful (about ½ cup) mint leaves

12 eggs

100 g unsalted butter

1 small handful chives, finely chopped

Lemon mascarpone cream

250 g mascarpone

finely grated zest of 1 lemon

salt flakes

ITELLO TONNATO

This dish is all about the tuna sauce, which we call *salsa tonnato*. You can buy it in jars in the supermarket in Italy, but of course it's better if you make it yourself. This is a very summery dish, great for picnics. It's easy to double the quantities to serve a crowd and any leftovers are delicious the next day as a *panino* (bread roll) filling – I love a *panino* with *salsa tonnato* and mortadella. We usually follow it with a fresh but filling cold minestrone, which is also very summery, and for me a *rosato* (rosé) wine is the perfect accompaniment. Lombardy, Piedmont and France argue about who invented this dish, but the name comes from the Lombardian dialect, *vitel tonne*, meaning 'tuna-flavoured veal'.

I use the girello cut (eye of round) of veal, which is a lean piece of meat normally incorporated with the rump. It's important to soak the capers well and to use a good-quality tuna preserved in olive oil; I like Campisi, an Italian brand available in Australia. If you happen to have a meat slicer, use it to slice the veal before serving.

Serves 6 as an entrée

1 × 500 g veal girello

6 sage leaves

1 fresh bay leaf

1 stalk pale inner celery heart

3 cloves

3 cups (750 ml) dry white wine

1 litre water

10 g rock salt

3 salted anchovy fillets

20 salted capers, rinsed and dried

vegetable oil, for deep-frying

freshly ground black pepper

Tonnato sauce

4 eggs, boiled for 8 minutes

250 g tinned tuna in olive oil, drained

1½ tablespoons extra virgin olive oil

1 teaspoon white wine vinegar

juice of ½ lemon, strained

Place the veal, sage, bay leaf, celery, cloves and wine in a heavy-based stainless-steel saucepan, then cover and refrigerate for 24 hours, turning the veal every 6 hours or so.

Remove the veal from the marinade and strain the liquid. Reserve the veal and liquid and discard the remaining solids. Return the veal and liquid to the pan, add the water and the salt and bring to the boil, then reduce the heat to low and simmer, covered, for 30 minutes. Add the anchovies and cook for another 10 minutes.

Remove the anchovies from the cooking liquid and set aside. Set the veal aside, in the liquid, covered, for 30 minutes.

To make the tonnato sauce, remove the yolks from the eggs, discarding the whites or reserving them for another purpose. Place the yolks, tuna, oil, vinegar, lemon juice and reserved anchovies in a blender and blend until smooth, adding a little of the veal cooking liquid if necessary to achieve a smooth consistency. Cover with plastic film and refrigerate until needed.

Heat vegetable oil for deep-frying in a small heavy-based saucepan and deep-fry the capers for 1 minute or until crisp, then drain on paper towel.

Slice the veal very thinly (about 1 mm thick), arrange on a platter and pour the tonnato sauce over the top. Sprinkle with pepper to taste, garnish with the capers and serve.

ATTUTA DI CERVO

VENISON TARTARE

The full name of this style of dish is *battuta al coltello*, meaning 'beat with a knife', but everyone just calls it *battuta*. This is a good way to prepare lean cuts of meat that would be too dry if you cooked them. It's a cousin of the French steak tartare, however, tartare is very finely chopped with a complex dressing, whereas the Italian version is cut a lot more coarsely and the dressing is very simple because we want to taste the meat. Ask your butcher to trim the membrane off the outside of the backstrap. I've also made this dish using kangaroo. Chestnut mustard fruit is available from specialist provedores, but if you can't find it, use another mustard fruit or make your own (see page 223). Amaranth seeds are available from health food stores. While they're not a traditional part of this dish, I like them because the nutty flavour and crisp texture lifts this to the next level. You can certainly make *battuta* without them, if you like. However, if you do use them, you really need a deep-frying thermometer (see page 227) – if the oil is too cold, the seeds won't puff up; if it's too hot, they'll burn.

Serves 6

500 g venison backstrap, trimmed
grapeseed oil, for deep-frying
1½ tablespoons (30 g)
    amaranth seeds
2 golden shallots, finely chopped
salt flakes
50 g chestnut mustard fruits
    (see page 225)
mustard micro-cress (optional),
    to serve

Mustard dressing
2 teaspoons strained lemon juice
1 tablespoon extra virgin olive oil
1 teaspoon Dijon mustard

To make the mustard dressing, place the lemon juice, oil and mustard in a screw-top jar and shake until emulsified. Add a little water if necessary to give the consistency of thickened cream.

Cut the venison into 5 mm dice and place in a large bowl, then set aside.

Heat grapeseed oil for deep-frying in a small heavy-based saucepan until it registers 205°C on a sugar/deep-fry thermometer (see page 227). Have a fine-mesh sieve ready over a stainless-steel bowl.

Drop half of the amaranth seeds into the hot oil; they will puff up immediately. Carefully pour the oil through the sieve into the bowl and set the amaranth seeds aside on paper towel to drain. Return the oil to the saucepan, reheat and repeat with the remaining amaranth seeds.

Add the shallot, salt to taste and dressing to the venison and, using your hands, mix well.

Scatter the venison mixture around a serving plate and arrange pieces of mustard fruit around the plate. Sprinkle the amaranth seeds and mustard cress, if using, over the top and serve.

NVOLTINI DI PESCE

BARRAMUNDI INVOLTINI

This dish is inspired by one I used to make when I worked at Fior di Roccia on Lake Garda. We laid out thin slices of raw fish (*crudo*) on a bed of radicchio, flashed it under the salamander (hot grill) to just cook it, then drizzled it with this dressing. You could also use salmon, tuna or swordfish, and I like this dressing drizzled on carpaccio. This is a good dish to prepare ahead of time for entertaining.

Serves 6

1 × 600 g sashimi-grade barramundi fillet, skin on, pin-boned

3 litres water

1 tablespoon rock salt

1 cup (200 g) arborio rice

50 ml extra virgin olive oil, plus extra for drizzling

1 tablespoon French tarragon leaves, finely chopped

1 small handful (about ¼ cup) chervil leaves, finely chopped

salt flakes and freshly ground white pepper

¼ radicchio, very finely shredded

chardonnay vinegar (see page 226), for drizzling

Olive dressing

75 g pitted Ligurian olives

100 ml extra virgin olive oil

Slice the fish on the diagonal into 18 thin slices, leaving the skin behind. Place three pieces slightly overlapping, on a piece of freezer film, top with another piece of film and gently pound with a kitchen mallet to form one even piece. Lift onto a plate with the film. Repeat with the remaining slices to give 6 flat pieces of overlapping fish. Stack them on top of each other and refrigerate.

Bring the water to the boil in a large heavy-based saucepan, then add the rock salt and rice and return to the boil. Reduce the heat to low and simmer for 15 minutes or until al dente. Drain the rice, toss with a little of the oil and spread on a tray, then refrigerate until cool.

Meanwhile, to make the olive dressing, combine the olives and oil in a jug and use a hand-held electric blender to finely chop. Set aside.

Stir most of the tarragon and chervil, the remaining oil and pepper to taste through the cooled rice. Taste and add salt if necessary.

Lay a sheet of plastic film on a workbench. Remove the top layer of freezer film, pick up the next sheet of film with the fish on it and turn it onto the plastic film on the workbench.

Place about 3 tablespoons of the rice mixture on the centre of the fish slice. Wrap the stuffed fish tightly in the plastic film, forming a cigar-shape. Place on a plate. Repeat with the remaining fish and rice mixture and refrigerate for at least 30 minutes.

Preheat the oven to 200°C.

Remove the plastic film and place the involtini, seam-side down, on a baking tray lined with baking paper. Drizzle with a little of the dressing.

Turn on the oven overhead grill function to high. Cook the involtini in the oven for 3 minutes or until warmed through and slightly coloured.

Dress the radicchio with a little of the olive dressing and a drizzle of vinegar. Spread the radicchio on a platter and arrange the involtini on top. Drizzle with the remaining dressing, sprinkle with the remaining tarragon and chervil, drizzle with extra oil and serve.

MONDEGHINI

BEEF MEATBALLS

These taste just like the ones my grandmother used to make! They are traditionally made with meat leftover from Bollito Misto (see page 173) or on the Monday after a Sunday roast, so feel free to use leftover meat if you have some in the refrigerator. In which case, you won't need to cook the meat first with the onion, celery and carrot, just chop it roughly. You can also make a tomato sauce, such as the one on page 55, to serve with the meatballs if you like. This recipe is all about using up the leftovers – the roast and the bread – it is real *cucina povera*.

Serves 6

1 × 200 g beef scotch fillet steak
½ carrot, roughly chopped
½ onion, roughly chopped
½ stalk celery, roughly chopped
salt flakes
50 g stale sourdough bread, diced
50 ml milk
75 g mortadella, roughly chopped
75 g Italian pork sausage meat
   (see page 225)
1 egg, lightly beaten
40 g Grana Padano, freshly grated
1 handful (about ½ cup) flat-leaf
   parsley leaves, roughly chopped
1 clove garlic, finely chopped
freshly ground black pepper
100 g fine fresh breadcrumbs
   (see page 226)
100 g unsalted butter, diced
100 ml extra virgin olive oil

Place the beef, carrot, onion, celery and salt in a heavy-based saucepan and add enough cold water to cover. Bring to the boil, then reduce the heat to low and simmer for 6–7 minutes or until the beef is cooked through. Remove from the heat and set aside in the saucepan to cool. Roughly chop the beef, discarding the liquid and vegetables.

Meanwhile, combine the bread and milk in a bowl and set aside for 10 minutes or until soft, then squeeze to remove the excess milk.

Place the beef, mortadella and sausage meat in a food processor and process until smooth. Transfer to a bowl and add the egg, Grana, parsley, garlic, bread and salt and pepper to taste. Stir to combine well. Using wet hands, form about 2 tablespoons of the mixture into an egg-shaped ball. Roll in the breadcrumbs and place on a tray. Repeat with the remaining beef mixture and breadcrumbs and refrigerate for at least 1 hour to firm.

Heat the butter and oil in a heavy-based frying pan over medium heat until foaming. Reduce the heat to low–medium, then, working in batches, fry the meatballs for 4 minutes on each side or until cooked through and well-coloured all over.

Sprinkle with salt and serve hot.

ACIADA

ONION AND TALEGGIO FOCACCIA

We traditionally eat this thin, light bread with salumi, but I like it just on its own. You can also serve it instead of regular bread, but it is heavier, and juicy and sweet from the onion. The focaccia dough is also sometimes filled with just cheese, such as taleggio, fontina or bitto; this is usually called *focaccia di lecco*. Some families use fruit, including peaches, figs or grapes, in their *focaccia di lecco* too. How much water you need to use will depend a lot on the flour, so just add it slowly until the dough has the right consistency. Make sure the water is at room temperature (about 25–30°C) – if it's too hot, it will kill the yeast. If you don't have a dough hook attachment for your electric mixer you can knead the dough by hand, but it's hard work. As the dough is very sticky, oil your hands before you handle it. If you use dried yeast instead of fresh yeast, you'll need to set the mixture aside for a few minutes to start to bubble after you've added the water.

Serves 6

25 g (5 teaspoons) fresh yeast or
  12 g dried yeast
150–250 ml lukewarm water,
  as needed
2 cups (300 g) plain flour
100 ml extra virgin olive oil
2 teaspoons fine salt
100 g taleggio, sliced
2 sprigs rosemary, leaves picked
salt flakes and freshly ground
  black pepper
caster sugar, for sprinkling

Onion topping
50 g unsalted butter
5 white onions, halved
  lengthways, thinly sliced
150 ml water

Dissolve the yeast with a little of the water in a small bowl.

Sift the flour into the bowl of an electric mixer fitted with a dough hook. Add the yeast mixture and, with the motor running on low speed, slowly drizzle in enough water to give a soft, sticky dough, you may not need all the water. Continue mixing for 15 minutes, adding a little extra water if the dough appears too dry; it should be soft and slightly sticky. Smear a little of the oil on top of the dough, cover with a clean tea towel and set aside in a warm place for 1 hour or until doubled in size.

Meanwhile, to make the onion topping, melt the butter in a heavy-based saucepan over high heat. Add the onion and reduce the heat to low, then cook for 5 minutes, stirring occasionally. Add the water and cook for 12–15 minutes or until the water has evaporated and the onion has softened and become lightly golden. Set aside to cool.

Add the remaining oil and salt to the dough and, using the dough hook, mix slowly for 5–10 minutes until all of the oil is incorporated. Wet a baking tray with a little water, then line with baking paper. Turn out the dough onto the tray and, using the tips of your fingers to dimple the dough, spread it into a 1 cm-thick oval. Top with the onion topping, taleggio, rosemary and salt and pepper to taste. Cover with a clean tea towel and set aside in a warm place for 1 hour.

Preheat the oven to 180°C.

Sprinkle the sugar over the top of the focaccia and bake for 40 minutes or until a wooden skewer inserted in the centre comes out clean.

FAGIOLI CON LE COTICHE
BORLOTTI BEANS WITH PORK SKIN

<u>Serves 4</u>

500 g pork skin, soaked in water
for 6 hours, then drained

2 small white onions, 1 roughly
chopped and 1 finely chopped

2 small carrots, 1 roughly
chopped and 1 finely chopped

2 stalks pale inner celery
heart, 1 roughly chopped
and 1 finely chopped

2 cloves garlic, 1 bruised
and 1 finely chopped

salt flakes

200 g dried borlotti beans, soaked
overnight in cold water

20 g lardo (see page
225), chopped

20 g unsalted butter

1 tablespoon extra virgin olive oil

50 g tomato paste (purée)

30 g Grana Padano, freshly grated

In the spaghetti westerns I grew up watching, there were two famous actors, Bud Spencer and Terence Hill, and in every movie Bud Spencer (the big one) was making the beans with the pork skin and Terence Hill would distract him and steal the beans while he wasn't looking. It always made me want to eat this dish, which my *Papà* called '*fagioli alla Terence Hill*'. You may need to order the pork skin in advance from your butcher. These days it usually comes already cleaned, but if not, burn any remaining hair off it and scrape it well with a sharp knife, then wash well on both sides and pat dry. You'll need to start this recipe a day ahead to give the beans time to soak. I also like to serve this as a side dish for meat, such as the Beef California-style (see picture on page 143).

Use a long sharp knife to cut the pork skin into strips about 7 cm × 3 cm.

Place the roughly chopped onion, carrot and celery in a large heavy-based saucepan, then add the skin, the bruised garlic and salt to taste. Cover with cold water and bring to the boil. Reduce the heat to low, then simmer, covered, for 40 minutes or until the skin is very tender. Drain, reserving the skin and the cooking liquid and discarding the vegetables. You will need 3 cups (750 ml) cooking liquid, so measure it and, if necessary, add enough water to yield this amount or discard any excess.

Meanwhile, drain the beans and place in a heavy-based saucepan. Add enough cold water to cover. Bring to the boil, then reduce the heat to low, cover and simmer for 40 minutes or until tender. Drain, discarding the liquid, and set aside.

Place the lardo, butter and oil in a heavy-based saucepan over medium heat. When the butter has melted, add the finely chopped onion, carrot, celery and garlic and cook for 5 minutes or until the vegetables have just started to colour. Stir in the tomato paste and season with salt to taste. Stir in the skin, beans and reserved cooking liquid. Reduce the heat to low, then cook, covered, for 30 minutes. Remove from the heat and set aside for 5 minutes.

Serve hot or warm in a flat bowl, topped with the Grana.

COSTE AL LATTE
SILVERBEET COOKED IN MILK

Serves 6

2 bunches (about 2 kg) silverbeet
salt flakes
100 g unsalted butter
2 tablespoons plain flour
300 ml full-cream milk
pinch of freshly grated nutmeg
25 g Grana Padano, freshly grated

My *nonna* used to cook silverbeet in the unpasteurised, unskimmed milk fresh from her cow – it was very rich in cream and made an unbelievable dish. So, don't be tempted to use skim or low-fat milk here; that just isn't the Lombardian way! This also works well as a side dish – try it alongside the Crumbed Veal Cutlets Milan-style (see picture on page 169).

Trim the leaves off the central stems of the silverbeet, discarding the stems.

Bring a large heavy-based saucepan of salted water to the boil. Working in batches, add the silverbeet, then return to the boil and boil for 3 minutes. Drain and place in iced water to cool, then squeeze well to remove any excess liquid. Roughly chop and set aside.

Melt 50 g of the butter in a heavy-based saucepan, then add the flour and cook for 3 minutes, whisking constantly. Whisk in the milk, bring to the boil, then reduce the heat to low and simmer, whisking constantly, for another 3 minutes or until thickened. Add the nutmeg and a good pinch of salt. Stir in the silverbeet, remaining butter and Grana.

Serve warm.

ASPARAGI MILANESE
ASPARAGUS WITH HARD-BOILED EGG

Serves 6

1.2 kg green asparagus spears,
   peeled (about 48)
salt flakes
8 eggs, hard-boiled
200 ml extra virgin olive oil
50 g Grana Padano, freshly grated
freshly ground black pepper

In Italy asparagus is cooked until it's tender – we don't serve it crisp. This is a recipe from my father's father, my *nonno* Bruno. It's traditionally served as a complete meal and is popular during Lent, when people usually abstain from eating meat, and when asparagus is in season in Europe. You could serve it as an entrée or side dish. When they're available, I use a mixture of green, white and purple asparagus for extra colour.

Trim the base of the asparagus so that they are all the same length.

Bring a large heavy-based saucepan of salted water to the boil, then add the asparagus and boil for 8 minutes or until tender. Drain and arrange on a platter.

Peel the eggs and roughly mash them, then mix in the oil, 25 g of the Grana and salt and pepper to taste. Spoon half of the egg mixture over the middle of the asparagus. Sprinkle the remaining Grana over the top and serve with the remaining egg mixture on the side for dipping.

FIORI DI ZUCCA RIPIENI
VEGETABLE-STUFFED ZUCCHINI FLOWERS

Serves 6

1 small (100 g) floury potato,
    such as russet or desiree,
    peeled and cut into 2 cm dice

100 g green beans, topped
    and tailed

1 green zucchini
    (courgette), halved

salt flakes

1 egg, lightly beaten

50 g Grana Padano, freshly grated

1 small clove garlic, finely chopped

1 tablespoon thinly sliced
    basil leaves

freshly ground black pepper

18 female zucchini (courgette)
    flowers, ends trimmed and
    stamens removed

25 g unsalted butter, melted

In Lombardy we bake rather than deep-fry stuffed zucchini flowers, as I've done here. We only deep-fry them without any filling, usually just dusted in flour.

Place the potato, beans and zucchini in a heavy-based saucepan of boiling salted water and boil for 15–20 minutes or until the potato is tender. Drain in a strainer and set aside to cool in the strainer.

Place the cooled vegetables in a food processor and process until smooth. Transfer to a large bowl and stir in the egg, Grana, garlic, basil and salt and pepper to taste. Refrigerate for at least 30 minutes to firm.

Preheat the oven to 180°C.

Place the vegetable mixture in a piping bag and pipe evenly into the centre of the zucchini flowers. Arrange the flowers in a single layer in a baking dish and brush with the butter, then sprinkle with salt and place on the centre shelf of the oven. Turn on the oven overhead grill function to high and grill for 10 minutes or until tender and ightly coloured, checking the flowers often as some grills are hotter than others.

Serve hot.

SCIATT
CHEESE IN BEER AND GRAPPA BATTER

Serves 8

1 cup (150 g) buckwheat flour
    (see page 225), sifted

¾ cup (110 g) plain flour, sifted

1 tablespoon grappa (see page 225)

fine salt

200 ml beer, chilled, as needed

grapeseed oil, for deep-frying

750 g fontina, cut into 2 cm dice
    and refrigerated

Sciatt means 'toad' in the Valtellina dialect, referring to the fact that these tasty strips of deep-fried cheese are ugly because of their dark colour and irregular shape. It's important to keep both the cheese and batter refrigerated until you are ready to start deep-frying.

Place the buckwheat and plain flours, grappa and salt to taste in a bowl. Gradually whisk in enough beer to form a smooth, thick batter; you may not need it all. Cover with plastic film and refrigerate for 1 hour.

Heat oil for deep-frying in a heavy-based saucepan or deep-fryer until it registers 180°C on a sugar/deep-fry thermometer (see page 227). Working in batches, use a spoon to dip pieces of the fontina into the batter and carefully place in the oil. Deep-fry for 1–2 minutes or until dark brown and crisp.

Drain on paper towel, sprinkle with salt and serve immediately.

FICHI IN PASTELLA RIPIENI DI TALEGGIO

TALEGGIO-FILLED FIGS IN BEER BATTER

This is a very traditional – and delicious – dish. It's a great combination of crisp and soft, sweet and savoury. Use ripe figs, but not so ripe that they fall apart when they're filled. You can stuff them with gorgonzola or goat's cheese instead of the taleggio if you like.

Serves 4

1 × 150 g piece taleggio, rind discarded, cut into cubes
8 large firm ripe figs
grapeseed oil, for deep-frying
plain flour, for dusting
salt flakes

Beer batter
1½ cups (225 g) plain flour, sifted
1 teaspoon fine salt
1½ cups (375 ml) beer, chilled, as needed

Place the taleggio in a bowl and mash with a fork until smooth, then place in a piping bag.

Make a small hole in the base of each fig with your finger and pipe in enough taleggio to plump up the fig; don't overfill or it will break when it's cooked.

To make the beer batter, place the flour and salt in a large bowl. Gradually whisk in enough beer to give the consistency of thickened cream; you may not need it all (it doesn't need to be perfectly smooth).

Immediately heat oil for deep-frying in a heavy-based saucepan or deep-fryer until it registers 180°C on a sugar/deep-fry thermometer (see page 227).

Dust the figs with flour, and, holding them by the stems, dip each one into the batter, then very carefully lower it into the hot oil (depending on the size of your fryer or saucepan, you might need to fry them in 2 batches so the oil temperature doesn't drop too much). Fry for 2–3 minutes or until golden brown, then drain on paper towel.

Sprinkle with salt and serve immediately so the batter doesn't soften.

RITTELLE DI BACCALÀ

SALT COD FRITTERS WITH CABBAGE SALAD

These fritters are deliciously light because they are based on a choux pastry. The mixture must be made at least two hours before it is cooked so it has time to rest, and it can be prepared up to a day in advance. You will need to start this recipe a day ahead to give the salt cod time to soak. This recipe makes about 25 fritters.

Serves 6

1 × 200 g piece salt cod (baccalà) fillet (see page 160)

1 desiree potato (about 75 g), peeled and diced

50 ml extra virgin olive oil

150 ml water

⅓ cup (50 g) plain flour

2 eggs

1 small handful (about ¼ cup) flat-leaf parsley leaves, finely chopped

grapeseed oil, for deep-frying

Cabbage salad

⅛ red cabbage (about 150 g), shredded

⅛ Savoy cabbage (about 150 g), shredded

¼ white onion, thinly sliced

salt flakes

extra virgin olive oil, for drizzling

Soak the salt cod in cold water for 24 hours, changing the water five times. Drain, then discard any skin or discoloured meat and roughly chop the remainder.

Bring a heavy-based saucepan of water to the boil and add the potato, then cook for 20 minutes or until very soft. Remove from the heat, add the salt cod to the pan, then cover and set aside.

Place the olive oil and water in a small heavy-based saucepan over medium heat and bring to the boil. Add the flour all at once and reduce the heat to low, then whisk vigorously until smooth. Cook for another 5 minutes, stirring often.

Drain the salt cod and potato, then place in a food processor and pulse until well combined but still slightly chunky. Set aside.

Transfer the flour mixture to a bowl, add an egg and whisk until smooth; the mixture will split when the egg is first added, but it will whisk back together. Repeat with the second egg. Stir in the potato and salt cod mixture and the parsley and cover, then refrigerate for at least 2 hours to firm.

Meanwhile, to make the cabbage salad, combine the cabbages and onion, sprinkle with salt to taste, drizzle with oil and toss well to combine. Arrange on a platter.

Heat grapeseed oil for deep-frying in a large heavy-based saucepan or deep-fryer until it registers 180°C on a sugar/deep-fry thermometer (see page 227).

Working in batches and using 2 dessertspoons, scoop up a spoonful of the salt cod mixture and use the second spoon to slide it into the hot oil. Deep-fry for 2–3 minutes or until golden. Drain on paper towel.

Place the fritters on top of the cabbage salad and serve immediately.

UMACHE DELLA ZIA BRUNA

AUNTY BRUNA'S SNAILS

Zia Bruna was my dad's aunty, and she was a great cook – one of the best in a family of great cooks. This is how she used to prepare snails, which are traditionally eaten in Lombardy. This aunty and her brother, my *nonno* Bruno, used to go up into the mountains after the rain and collect the snails, then keep them in a bird cage for three days. During this time, they'd feed them on polenta to purge them. Here in Australia I buy snails from Snails Bon Appetite in the Hunter Valley (they sell cooked cryovacked ones by mail order: snails.com.au), but I've also used tinned snails when I haven't been able to get fresh ones. It's important to cook the snails and vegetables until they start to stick a little and you get a brown layer on the base of the pan – this is where all the flavour is. When you add the wine and dissolve these caramelised brown bits all that flavour goes into the sauce. If I was serving this dish as a *primo*, I'd serve it with soft polenta (see page 49).

Serves 6

½ bunch (about 500 g) silverbeet

2 tablespoons extra virgin olive oil

100 g unsalted butter

1 large onion, finely chopped

1 stalk pale inner celery heart, finely chopped

2 cloves garlic, finely chopped

500 g cooked snail meat, each snail cut in half

salt flakes

50 ml dry white wine

8 tinned whole, peeled Italian tomatoes, chopped

300 ml water

2 large handfuls (about 2 cups) flat-leaf parsley leaves, roughly chopped

40 g Grana Padano, freshly grated

1 egg, lightly beaten

crusty bread, to serve

Cut the stalks off the silverbeet and discard. Cut the green leaves off the remaining central stalks. Thinly slice the leaves and chop the stalks.

Place the oil and 50 g of the butter in a heavy-based saucepan over medium heat. When the butter melts, add the onion, celery, garlic and silverbeet stalk. Increase the heat to high and cook for 2–3 minutes or until lightly coloured. Add the snails to the onion mixture and cook for 5 minutes or until the mixture starts to stick and the base of the pan browns a little. Add salt to taste and the wine and stir well to remove any bits stuck to the bottom of the pan. Stir in the tomato and cook for another couple of minutes or until some of the liquid has evaporated. Add the silverbeet leaves and the water, then cook, covered, for 30 minutes, stirring occasionally.

Remove from the heat and set aside for at least 10 minutes. (You can prepare to this stage up to a day in advance, refrigerate and reheat just before serving.)

When ready to serve, stir through the parsley, remaining butter, the Grana and salt to taste, then the egg, which will cook in the residual heat, thickening the sauce slightly. Serve hot, with bread on the side.

ZUPPE E MINESTRE

SOUP

My *nonna* served soup between the antipasto and *primo* to *aprire lo stomaco* ('open the stomach'). It was also a way to ensure nothing was wasted – stale bread became dumplings boiled in leftover poaching liquid to create a dish that may not look pretty but was warming and delicious! *Zuppa* tends to be more vegetable-based, while *minestra* is heartier, usually with some pasta, gnocchi or rice added. And remember, don't serve soup piping hot or you'll dull the flavours.

MINESTRA MARICONDA
SOUP WITH BREAD GNOCCHI

Serves 8

300 g sourdough bread, crusts
   discarded, roughly chopped
2 cups (500 ml) milk
100 g unsalted butter, melted
4 eggs
150 g Grana Padano,
   freshly grated
⅔ cup (100 g) plain flour, sifted
1 pinch of freshly grated nutmeg
salt flakes and freshly ground
   black pepper
2 litres Beef Stock (see page 221)

This very old recipe is related to similar recipes for using up stale bread from neighbouring Tirol and Switzerland, where the dumplings are called *knudle*. I like this simple, comforting soup – it's just what I crave when I'm a bit under the weather.

Place the bread and milk in a bowl and leave to soak for at least 30 minutes, then squeeze to remove the excess milk. Place the bread in a mixing bowl and stir through the butter. Add the eggs, 100 g of the Grana, the flour, nutmeg and salt and pepper to taste. Mix to combine well. Cover and refrigerate for 1 hour.

Shape the mixture into 2 cm balls. Bring the stock to the boil in a large heavy-based saucepan. Working in batches, add the balls, and cook for 2–3 minutes or until they float to the surface. Scoop them out, then arrange in soup bowls.

Divide the boiling stock among the bowls, sprinkle with the remaining Grana and serve.

ZUPPA DI CIPOLLE
ONION SOUP

Serves 6

70 g unsalted butter
1 kg onions, thinly sliced
⅓ cup (50 g) plain flour
3 sage leaves, chopped
salt flakes and freshly ground
   black pepper
50 ml dry white wine
1.3 litres Chicken Stock (see
   page 222)
150 g Grana Padano,
   freshly grated

Crostini
12 thin slices ciabatta
extra virgin olive oil, for drizzling
salt flakes

This dish is similar to French onion soup, only lighter. This isn't surprising given that it was the cooks of an Italian princess – Caterina de' Medici, who married King Henry II of France – that taught the household staff of the French court how to cook!

Melt the butter in a large heavy-based saucepan over low heat. Stir in the onion and cook, covered, stirring occasionally, for 50 minutes or until soft and lightly coloured. Add the flour, sage and salt and pepper to taste and cook for another 4 minutes. Add the wine and cook for 2–3 minutes or until it has evaporated.

Add the stock and return to the boil, then reduce the heat to low and simmer, covered, for another 1 hour, stirring occasionally. Remove from the heat, keep covered and set aside.

Meanwhile, to make the crostini, preheat the oven to 180°C.

Place the bread on a baking tray, drizzle with a little oil, sprinkle with salt to taste and bake for 15 minutes or until crisp and golden. Set aside.

Whisk the Grana into the soup, ladle into bowls and serve with the crostini on the side.

Soup with bread gnocchi

UPPA ALLA PAVESE

POACHED EGG IN CHICKEN BROTH

Traditionally this dish is made by pouring boiling stock over an uncooked egg and toasted bread, so the egg stays quite raw and the toast soaks up the stock and falls apart – it's hearty and rustic. In my slightly more refined version, diners break the poached egg open in the soup and stir it through, then add the croutons at the table just before eating, which gives a lovely contrasting crunch.

Serves 4

50 g unsalted butter

150 g sourdough bread, crusts discarded, cut into 1 cm cubes

1 litre Chicken Stock (see page 222)

1 tablespoon white wine vinegar

4 eggs

50 g Grana Padano, freshly grated

Melt the butter in a heavy-based saucepan over high heat until foaming. Add the bread and reduce the heat to low, then cook, stirring, for 5 minutes or until the bread is crisp and golden. Tip the croutons onto paper towel to drain.

Place the stock in a heavy-based saucepan and bring to the boil. Reduce the heat to low, then simmer, covered, until ready to serve.

Meanwhile, bring a deep heavy-based frying pan, three-quarters full of water, to a gentle simmer over medium heat and stir in the vinegar. One by one, break each egg into a cup, gently slide it into the water, reduce the heat to low–medium and poach for 2 minutes. Using a slotted spoon, carefully lift the eggs out of the water and drain well, then place each one in a soup bowl.

Gently divide the hot stock among the bowls, then sprinkle with the croutons and Grana and serve.

L'ORZATA

BARLEY SOUP

This thick hearty soup is perfect for cold northern Italy. It is even better made a day ahead and reheated; though you may need to add a little extra stock or water to thin it out when you warm it. In Milan, they call this dish *l'urgiada*, but it's essentially the same. You'll need to start this recipe the day before to give the barley and beans time to soak. Soak them separately, as you don't add them to the soup at the same time. If you're short on time, use 400 g tinned borlotti beans and bring the barley to the boil, then leave it to soak in the pan of hot water for an hour or two. And don't worry if the milk in the soup splits – it often does, but will still taste good.

Place the oil, onion, leek, salt to taste and pancetta in a large heavy-based saucepan over high heat and cook, stirring often, for 10 minutes or until the onion is soft, lightly coloured and just starting to stick to the pan.

Drain and rinse the barley and borlotti beans, keeping them separate. Add the barley to the pan and stir for 1 minute. Add enough of the water to just cover, then bring to the boil. Add the milk and salt to taste and return to the boil, then add the beans and potato. Return to the boil and reduce the heat to low, then cover and simmer for 1 hour, stirring often; it should have a thick, soupy consistency, but if it becomes too thick, add a little water. Remove from the heat, stir in the Grana, cover and set aside for an hour or so.

When ready to serve, reheat over low heat, ladle into a tureen or individual bowls, drizzle with olive oil and sprinkle with extra Grana.

Serves 8

50 ml extra virgin olive oil, plus extra for drizzling

1 white onion, finely chopped

1 leek, white part only, washed well and finely chopped

salt flakes

1 × 80 g piece pancetta, finely diced

150 g pearl barley, soaked overnight in cold water

150 g dried borlotti beans, soaked overnight in cold water

2 cups (500 ml) water, as needed

1 litre milk

1 desiree potato (about 180 g), peeled and diced

50 g Grana Padano, freshly grated, plus extra for serving

PANADA

GRATED BREAD SOUP

When I was at school, I had lunch with my grandfather twice a week, and he always made this soup followed by the Asparagus with Hard-boiled Egg on page 25. This is a hearty soup and we'd eat a kilo of asparagus between us, then watch the news together. *Nonno* always ended up snoozing at the table and I'd be left watching TV. I remember he was often asleep at the dining table – he'd eat his dinner then sometimes nod off in his chair until two in the morning. He was in the Italian army during WWII, endimg up in a POW camp in Germany when Italy changed sides. *Nonno* escaped and walked from Germany back to Italy, working as a cook for the American army in France along the way. No one heard from him for about three years, then one day he just wandered back into our village square. He was my idol and, when I was young, I loved hearing about his exploits. We still discuss *Nonno*'s adventures whenever we sit together as a family to eat.

Serves 6

1 cup (70 g) fine fresh breadcrumbs (see page 226)

1.5 litres Chicken Stock (see page 222)

70 g unsalted butter

3 eggs

50 g Grana Padano, freshly grated

salt flakes and freshly ground black pepper

Put ½ cup (35 g) of the breadcrumbs in a small bowl and stir in ½ cup (125 ml) of the stock. Melt 35 g of the butter in a small heavy-based frying pan over medium heat. Add the wet breadcrumbs and stir for 2–3 minutes or until lightly coloured.

Meanwhile, bring the remaining stock to the boil in a heavy-based saucepan.

Place the eggs, Grana, all the breadcrumbs, and salt and pepper to taste in a bowl and whisk together. Whisk the breadcrumb mixture into the boiling stock over medium heat and return to the boil, then reduce the heat to low and cook for 15 minutes. Stir in the remaining butter, ladle into bowls and serve.

# SBROFADEI IN BRODO

CHICKEN BROTH WITH PASTA

Variations of this dish are cooked throughout Lombardy and neighbouring Emilia Romagna. In Italy, ingredients such as onion and garlic are often chopped together to form a flavour base (called *battuto*, meaning 'beat'). It's important that they're all chopped together, not just chopped separately then combined because this helps meld the flavours before they even hit the pan. The *battuto* is fried to make a *soffritto*, which flavours the soup like a stock cube. This very tasty dish was traditionally made by the poor people on the plain of Mantua using just water, not stock, as the *soffritto* provided the flavour – you can easily make a vegetarian version by following their lead. Traditionally the stock was made as a way to use up a capon (castrated male chicken), but they can be hard to buy so use a good free-range chicken instead.

Serves 4

1.6 litres Chicken Stock (see page 222)
50 g Grana Padano, freshly grated

Pasta dough
1 egg
2 egg yolks
50 g Grana Padano, freshly grated
pinch of freshly grated nutmeg
salt flakes
⅔ cup (100 g) 00 flour (see page 225), plus extra for dusting

To make the pasta dough, break the egg into a bowl, add the yolks and beat lightly with a fork. Stir in the Grana, nutmeg and salt to taste, then slowly sift in the flour, stirring to form a firm dough. Tip onto a clean, dry workbench lightly dusted with flour and knead until smooth, then wrap in plastic film and refrigerate for 1–2 hours to rest.

Place the stock in a heavy-based saucepan and bring to the boil.

Push the dough, in batches, through a potato ricer into the boiling stock, using a sharp knife dipped in the boiling stock to cut the pieces of pasta off the base of the ricer, then stirring with a wooden spoon to separate them. Boil for 1 minute or until the pasta floats to the surface.

Remove from the heat. Ladle the broth and pasta into bowls, sprinkle with the Grana and serve.

MINESTRONE ALLA BRIANZOLA

VEGETABLE SOUP FROM BRIANZOLA

Lombardian tradition dictates that nothing is wasted in the kitchen, so we usually add the rind of the Grana to this soup. Some delicatessens and cheesemongers will sell it, or you can save it when you grate Grana or parmesan for another dish. For a vegetarian version, leave out the pork skin, which may need to be ordered in advance from your butcher.

Serves 6

400 g fresh borlotti beans, shelled

1½ tablespoons extra virgin olive oil

2 zucchinis (courgettes), finely chopped

3 carrots, finely chopped

1 white onion, finely chopped

2 stalks celery, finely chopped

100 g lardo (see page 225), chopped

150 g pork skin, soaked in water for 6 hours, then drained and sliced

1 clove garlic, finely chopped

3 roma (plum) tomatoes, peeled and chopped

2 sage leaves

3 litres water

½ Savoy cabbage, thinly sliced

3 desiree potatoes, peeled and finely diced

1 cup (200 g) carnaroli rice (see page 225)

150 g Grana Padano, freshly grated

1½ tablespoons thinly sliced sage

Place the beans in a heavy-based saucepan of water and bring to the boil. Reduce the heat to low and simmer for 40 minutes or until tender. Drain and set aside.

Heat the oil in a large heavy-based saucepan over low heat. Add the zucchini, carrot, onion, celery, lardo, pork skin and garlic, then cook, covered, for 6 minutes. Add the tomato, sage and beans and cook for another 10 minutes.

Add the water and bring to the boil, then reduce the heat to low and simmer, stirring occasionally, for 30 minutes. Add the cabbage and cook, stirring occasionally, for another hour. Add the potato and rice and return to the boil, then reduce the heat to low and cook for another 25 minutes or until the potato and rice are tender.

Ladle into soup bowls, sprinkle with the Grana and sage and serve.

POLENTA
AND
RISOTTO

When I was growing up we ate polenta at virtually every meal. In the mountains, where it's too cold to grow wheat for bread, a porridge of buckwheat (*polenta taragna*, see page 50) has always been our staple. When corn arrived from the New World, it was ground and cooked in the same way, and sometimes we mix the two. Rice also grows well on the fertile plains of our Po Valley, making it the home of risotto – a dish I am very passionate about!

OLENTA

SOFT POLENTA

In China it's rice, in Ireland it's potatoes, and in Lombardy it's polenta that appears on the table at seemingly just about every meal. I like to use a coarse polenta from the town of Storo, which is just across the border in the region of Trentino, as it has a lovely, nutty flavour. Soak the saucepan and whisk in cold water as soon as you take the polenta out of the pan so that they're easier to wash later. If you like, make a well in the centre of the polenta in the serving bowl and pour in some of the cooking juices from whatever you're serving with it. This method is the same for both yellow (see picture on page 161), and white polenta (see picture on page 157). However, white polenta only takes about 30 minutes to cook.

Serves 8 as a side dish

2 litres cold water
20 g fine salt
450 g polenta

Combine the water and salt in a large heavy-based saucepan and bring to the boil. Whisking constantly, slowly 'rain' in the polenta. Reduce the heat to low and continue cooking, stirring frequently, for 1 hour or until the polenta is so thick that it starts to come away from the side of the pan. Transfer to a bowl and serve.

POLENTA TARAGNA

BUCKWHEAT POLENTA WITH SAUSAGE AND GORGONZOLA

On the first day we were in Lombardy to research this book, I took Roberta and Franz up to the hunting lodge owned by my family friends Elsa and Tulio, where Elsa and my mum made this polenta over an open fire in the garden. Cooked like this, or even in a copper pot over a wood fire in the house, which *Mamma* did when I was growing up, the polenta takes on a subtle smokiness. This is the traditional way and gives the best flavour. This type of polenta is traditionally served as a full meal, not just a side dish. If you want to serve it as a side dish, it'll serve ten to twelve people.

Serves 8 as a main

2.5 litres water

1 tablespoon fine salt

600 g buckwheat polenta
  (see page 225)

100 g unsalted butter

400 g Italian pork sausage meat
  (see page 225)

1 handful sage, leaves picked

200 g gorgonzola

150 g Grana Padano,
  freshly grated

Combine the water and salt in a large heavy-based saucepan and bring to the boil. Whisking constantly, slowly 'rain' in the polenta. Reduce the heat to low and continue cooking, stirring frequently, for 45 minutes.

After 45 minutes, continue cooking the polenta, but also heat the butter in a heavy-based frying pan over medium heat for 4–5 minutes or until it starts foaming. Add the sausage meat and sage to the pan and cook for 12 minutes or until the sausage meat is cooked through and crumbly.

Stir half the sausage meat into the polenta and add the gorgonzola, then cook for another 5 minutes or until the gorgonzola has melted. Add 100 g of the Grana and stir until melted.

Transfer to a serving bowl or divide among plates, arrange the remaining sausage mixture on top, sprinkle with the remaining Grana and serve.

POLENTA DI GRANO SARACENO CON FUNGHI TRIFOLATI

BUCKWHEAT POLENTA WITH MUSHROOMS

Grano saraceno is the Italian name for buckwheat, literally 'Saracen's grain', as buckwheat was introduced to Italy by the Turks. It's best to make this dish in autumn, when there's a good choice of wild mushrooms. I like using a mixture of slippery jacks, chestnut mushrooms and pine mushrooms, but use whatever you can find. Gorgonzola piccante is the original gorgonzola, with a sharper flavour than the now more common gorgonzola dolce. While polenta is usually a side dish, adding these mushrooms, with their rich, almost meaty flavour, transforms this into a satisfying meal in itself. You could serve a salad with it, if you like.

Serves 6 as a main

2 litres water

1½ tablespoons fine salt

500 g buckwheat polenta
  (see page 225)

50 g unsalted butter

50 g dried porcini mushrooms,
  soaked in water until soft,
  drained

200 g mixed mushrooms,
  thinly sliced

1 clove garlic, bruised

1 small handful (about ¼ cup)
  flat-leaf parsley leaves,
  thinly sliced

150 g gorgonzola piccante, diced

100 g Grana Padano,
  freshly grated

Combine the water and salt in a large heavy-based saucepan and bring to the boil. Whisking constantly, slowly 'rain' in the polenta. Reduce the heat to low and continue cooking, stirring frequently, for 1 hour or until the polenta is so thick that it starts to come away from the side of the pan.

When the polenta is almost ready, melt the butter in a heavy-based frying pan over high heat. Add the porcini, mixed mushrooms and garlic and cook for 5 minutes or until well coloured. Remove the garlic, then stir in the parsley.

When the polenta is ready, stir in the gorgonzola and Grana and cook for another 2 minutes.

Spoon the polenta onto a large wooden board or into a wide shallow bowl, arrange the mushrooms on top, pour over the butter and serve.

POLENTA DI PATATE
'POLENTA' OF POTATO

Serves 8 as a side dish

1 kg russet or other floury
    potatoes, scrubbed
fine salt
2 tablespoons extra virgin olive oil
150 g unsalted butter
3 cloves garlic, bruised
200 ml tomato passata
25 g Grana Padano, freshly grated

Lombardians love their polenta so much that even a dish like this, that doesn't contain any corn, is still called 'polenta' because that's what it looks like. It has quite a sticky, polenta-like texture from the working of the starch in the potato. Because it's quite a wet dish it works well as an accompaniment to dry dishes like sausages or grilled meats, as well as wet dishes such as the Venison Braised in Red Wine (see picture on page 175).

Place the potatoes in a large heavy-based saucepan, cover with water, add the salt and bring to the boil. Reduce the heat to low and simmer for 30–40 minutes or until a wooden skewer can be inserted into a potato without any resistance.

Meanwhile, place the oil and 50 g of the butter in a heavy-based saucepan over medium heat until the butter melts. Add the garlic and cook for 2 minutes, then add the tomato passata and cook for 7 minutes or until the mixture thickens a little. Discard the garlic.

Drain the potatoes and press through a potato ricer into the tomato mixture, whisking the potato into the sauce to make a smooth purée. Whisk in salt to taste, the remaining butter and the Grana, then transfer to a serving bowl and serve.

POLENTA ALLA GRIGLIA
GRILLED POLENTA

Serves 8 as a side dish

1 quantity Soft Polenta (see
    page 49)
extra virgin olive oil, for brushing

When I grew up we generally ate polenta every day. The first day we'd eat it soft (see page 49), then the second day *Mamma* would serve the leftovers grilled. Even now, if we have the charcoal grill already going to cook sausages, chicken or mushrooms, for example, then we just throw some slices of leftover set polenta onto the grill as well. Sometimes we drizzle *pestatina*, a fresh sauce made by mixing chopped garlic and parsley with olive oil, over the polenta and grilled meats. I especially like this, alongside the Stuffed Baked Barramundi (see picture on page 131).

Spread out the polenta on a shallow tray to a depth of 2 cm and refrigerate until firm.

Turn the polenta out onto a clean, dry workbench and slice into squares. Brush the squares with oil.

Preheat a barbecue grill plate or chargrill pan to medium–high heat. Grill the squares for 3–4 minutes each side, until they have a nice crust.

POLENTA AL FORNO
BAKED POLENTA WITH TOMATO SAUCE

Serves 8 as a side dish or entrée

1 quantity Soft Polenta (see
   page 49)

160 g Grana Padano,
   freshly grated

64 artichoke quarters preserved
   in oil

Tomato sauce

1 tablespoon extra virgin olive oil

1 small red onion, finely diced

2 cloves garlic, finely chopped

800 g tinned whole, peeled
   Italian tomatoes

This is another great way to use up leftover soft polenta – just spread it out on a baking tray to a depth of about 2 cm to set, then bake it the next day. Of course, you could also make the polenta fresh, spread it on a tray and refrigerate it for just a couple of hours to set. I like to make this whenever I cook my Mascarpone-filled Guinea Fowl (see picture on page 155).

To make the tomato sauce, heat the oil in a heavy-based frying pan over medium heat. Add the onion and garlic and cook for 2–3 minutes or until translucent. Add the tomatoes and crush with a wooden spoon. Bring to the boil, then reduce the heat to low and simmer for 15 minutes or until the tomatoes have broken down and the sauce has thickened slightly.

Meanwhile, preheat the oven to 200°C. Wet a baking tray with a little water, then line with baking paper.

While the sauce is simmering, turn the polenta out onto a clean, dry workbench and, using an 8 cm round cutter, cut out 16 discs. Arrange the discs in a single layer on the lined tray, sprinkle evenly with 80 g of the Grana and top each disc with 4 artichoke quarters, then sprinkle evenly with the remaining Grana.

Turn on the oven grill function to high.

Place the tray in the oven and cook under the hot grill for 8–10 minutes or until the cheese is golden-brown, watching it closely; if the tops start to brown too quickly, turn off the overhead grill.

Spread the tomato sauce onto a serving platter, top with the polenta discs and serve.

ARGOTTINI ALLA BERGAMASCA

EGG YOLK-FILLED SEMOLINA TIMBALE WITH MUSHROOM SAUCE

The semolina for this dish is cooked in a similar way to polenta. It's important to 'rain' it into the water, whisking all the time so it doesn't go lumpy. This timbale is traditionally made in one large mould (called a *margotta*) for the whole table to share, although I've made individual serves here. I like to use pine mushrooms for the sauce if they're in season – chestnut mushrooms, Swiss browns, oyster mushrooms, slippery jacks and enoki are all good too.

Serves 8 as an entrée

1 litre Chicken Stock (see page 222)

300 g fine semolina

fine salt

70 g unsalted butter, plus extra for buttering

30 g Grana Padano, freshly grated

freshly ground white pepper

200 g gruyère, thinly sliced

8 egg yolks

Mushroom sauce

½ cup (125 ml) extra virgin olive oil

60 g unsalted butter

1 clove garlic, bruised

1 onion, finely chopped

350 g mixed mushrooms, trimmed and cut into bite-sized pieces

⅓ cup (85 g) tomato passata

½ teaspoon dried oregano

1 small handful (about ¼ cup) flat-leaf parsley leaves, finely chopped

salt flakes and freshly ground black pepper

Bring the stock to the boil in a heavy-based saucepan. Whisking constantly, slowly 'rain' in the semolina. Add salt to taste, then reduce the heat to low and continue cooking, stirring frequently, for 15 minutes or until the semolina is so thick that it starts to come away from the side of the pan. Remove from the heat, stir in the butter, Grana and pepper to taste and set aside to cool a little.

Meanwhile, generously butter eight 150 ml-capacity timbale moulds or ramekins and refrigerate until needed.

Using a 4.5 cm round cutter, cut out 16 rounds from the gruyère.

Preheat the oven to 220°C.

Place a 2 cm layer of semolina in the bottom of each mould. Press a disc of gruyere into the centre of each mould, making an indentation in the middle of the semolina. Carefully place an egg yolk on top of the gruyère and top with another disc of gruyere. Fill the moulds with the remaining semolina, ensuring the egg yolks are completely encased.

Place the moulds on a baking tray and bake for 15 minutes, putting the oven overhead grill function on for the last couple of minutes, until the tops are lightly coloured. Set aside to rest for a few minutes.

Meanwhile, to make the mushroom sauce, heat a heavy-based frying pan over high heat. Add the oil and butter and, when the butter melts, add the garlic and onion and cook for 3 minutes or until soft. Add the mushrooms and stir for 2 minutes. Add the passata and cook for 1 minute, then stir in the oregano, parsley and salt and pepper to taste. Remove from the heat, discard the garlic, then cover and set aside to keep warm.

Unmould each timbale onto a wide spatula or egg lift, then carefully turn over and place on a bowl or plate. Spoon the sauce around them and serve.

56

POLENTA

The word 'polenta' comes from the Latin for 'hulled barley' and refers to a thick porridge that today is most commonly made from white or yellow cornmeal. This wasn't always the case though, as corn was one of the many foods Christopher Columbus brought back to Europe from The Americas in the 16th century. Before that, polenta *taragna* (see page 50), made from the local buckwheat, was the staple on the Lombardian table. Today we still enjoy buckwheat polenta and sometimes also use a mixture of cornmeal and buckwheat.

Polenta is more than a side dish – in a land where winters are harsh and food was often scarce, it could form the basis of an entire family meal. Traditionally cooked over an open fire and stirred with a long wooden stick called *canna della polenta*, it was poured onto the centre of the wooden kitchen table with a simple sauce poured into the middle. The family sat around and took some of each from the table directly onto their plate; these days this is often replicated with polenta poured onto a large wooden board in the middle of the table.

Leftover polenta is versatile and never wasted. It sets firmly when cold and is often either baked in the oven or sliced and grilled to form a side dish or snack for the next day. My favourite cornmeal for polenta is polenta *di storo*, which is not produced in Lombardy but just across the border in our neighbouring region, Trentino-Alto Adige. It's quite coarse and takes a long time to cook out – but it is well worth the effort. Good polenta can't be rushed – you have to take the time to cook the cornmeal, stirring often until it is tender. The flavour is infinitely better than what you'll get if you use the precooked 'instant polenta'.

RISOTTO

We're crazy for risotto in Lombardy and, although it's now made all over Italy, the best risotto rice grows in our Po Valley, and risotto is treated with great reverence in the Lombardian kitchen. We believe when risotto is plated, no grain of rice should be on top of another otherwise it will overcook from the residual heat – the risotto should lie flat on the plate so that all the grains cool equally. To achieve this, the finished risotto must be quite wet: 'wave-like' or *all'onda* in Italian. It is always served on a flat plate and we tap the bottom of the plate firmly to smooth the risotto out. Different regions make risotto in different styles, for example in neighbouring Piedmont they mound it up on the plate. We call this style of dish *risi*, not risotto (see the Chicken Rice on page 69 and Rice with Pork Sausage on page 71).

There are different species of risotto rice: although arborio is the most widely available it's not the best, and vialone nano (the risotto rice of choice in Venice) is used to make *risi* in Lombardy, but rarely for risotto. For me, the best rice is carnaroli, specifically one that's been aged for one to ten years. Grains of carnaroli have the capacity to absorb more liquid, therefore more flavour, without splitting. The aging process is important too, because as rice ages it dries out, which means when it's cooked it can absorb more liquid (and more flavour). Every container of rice is different. When I first open a tin, I find the rice needs to cook for a little longer than rice from a tin that's been open for a few days – I think it starts to absorb humidity from the air as soon as it's opened. Because of this, and as the temperature of every stove (and therefore the rate of evaporation) also varies, the cooking time and stock quantity for a risotto recipe can't be precise.

Good risotto isn't hard to make – it just requires patiently following three simple steps. First comes *tostatura*, toasting the grains of rice in the oil until they smell slightly nutty. The most patience is required during the middle step. Despite what many people say, the secret to a good risotto is to NOT stir it at first. Just keep adding more stock as the grains soak it up and, as long as you don't start to stir, the rice won't stick. Once you start stirring, then you must keep stirring until the risotto is cooked – I only start to stir once the rice is half cooked. The final step, *mantacatura*, is the vigorous beating of butter and cheese into the risotto to make it creamy.

The most basic risotto is Parmesan Risotto (see page 62). Use this recipe (without the red wine reduction and mushrooms) as a starting point to make whatever variations you like – add gorgonzola or taleggio instead of the parmesan, or stir in herbs, seafood or your favourite green vegetables, for example.

ISOTTO ALLA MILANESE

RISOTTO MILANESE

I learnt to cook this classic dish when I worked for renowned chef Gualtiero Marchesi – who garnishes his version with edible gold leaf – but this is my own version. This is the traditional accompaniment to Ossibuchi (see picture on page 151); that's why it contains bone marrow. However, butchers will generally sell just the bone marrow already removed from the bones if you aren't making ossibuchi. You can just serve this as a simple risotto course, as with all of the risottos in this chapter.

Serves 6

2 litres Chicken Stock
   (see page 222)

25 g unsalted butter

450 g (about 2¼ cups) carnaroli
   rice (see page 225)

salt flakes

1 pinch of saffron threads

25 g veal bone marrow
   (order from your butcher),
   finely chopped

75 g cold Acid Butter
   (see page 224)

50 g Grana Padano, freshly grated

Place the stock in a heavy-based saucepan over high heat and bring to a simmer, then reduce the heat to low and cover.

Melt the unsalted butter in a deep heavy-based frying pan over medium heat. Add the rice and a pinch of salt and cook, stirring constantly, for 2–3 minutes or until very hot but not coloured; it should start to smell toasty. Add the saffron and enough stock to just cover the rice and cook for 8 minutes, adding more stock a ladle at a time as each ladleful is absorbed, shaking the pan to combine; do not stir. After 8 minutes, start stirring. Cook for another 7–9 minutes or until the rice is al dente, adding more stock as needed and stirring constantly. Remove the pan from the heat, cover and set aside for 1 minute.

Add the bone marrow, acid butter and Grana and, using a wooden spoon and shaking the pan, beat to create a creamy consistency, adding a little more stock if necessary to get the right consistency.

Spoon onto flat plates and tap each plate gently on a tea towel-covered workbench to flatten out the risotto. Serve.

ISOTTO AL SALTO

CRISP RICE CAKES

This dish was invented as a way to use up leftover risotto, but it's become a famous dish in its own right and is usually made with Risotto Milanese, although you could use any leftover risotto you have on hand. It's great on its own or as an accompaniment to any braised meat, poultry or seafood, as the crisp cake soaks up all the delicious sauce – for example, it's the perfect accompaniment to my Beef with Anchovy and Olive Oil (see picture on page 147).

Serves 4 as a side dish

olive oil, for cooking
400 g Risotto Milanese
(see opposite)

Preheat the oven to 100°C.

Heat a drizzle of oil in a heavy-based frying pan over medium heat. Add 100 g of the risotto, pressing it into the pan with the back of a large metal spoon to form a flat rice cake. Cook for 4 minutes, then use a spatula to loosen the side and shake the pan gently to start to loosen the bottom. Cook for another 6–8 minutes, loosening the side of the rice cake and shaking the pan occasionally, until it moves freely.

Place a large plate over the top of the frying pan and turn the rice cake out onto the plate. Slide it back into the pan and cook the other side for another 4 minutes or so, shaking gently from time to time to loosen it. Transfer to an ovenproof serving plate and place in the oven to keep hot. Repeat with the remaining risotto and oil as needed to make three more cakes. Serve.

RISOTTO ALLA PARMIGANA CON FUNGHI TRIFOLATI

PARMESAN RISOTTO AND MUSHROOMS WITH GARLIC AND PARSLEY

Only make this dish in autumn when wild mushrooms are available; it won't taste the same if made with just cultivated mushrooms. *Trifolati* is a style of cooking where an ingredient, often mushrooms but sometimes zucchini, artichoke or eggplant, is tossed quickly in a frying pan with garlic, parsley and olive oil.

Serves 6

2 litres Chicken Stock
  (see page 222)
85 g unsalted butter
450 g (about 2¼ cups) carnaroli
  rice (see page 225)
salt flakes
35 g cold Acid Butter (see page 224)
50 g Grana Padano, freshly grated
extra virgin olive oil, for drizzling

Red-wine reduction

30 g cold unsalted butter, diced
½ small white onion, finely chopped
3 cups (750 ml) red wine
¼ cup (60 ml) Brown Stock
  (see page 220)
½ teaspoon caster sugar

Mushrooms with garlic and parsley

60 g unsalted butter
1½ tablespoons extra virgin
  olive oil
1 clove garlic, bruised
100 g each slippery jack and pine
  mushrooms, cut into eighths
100 g chestnut mushrooms
salt flakes
1 handful (about ½ cup) flat-leaf
  parsley leaves, finely chopped

To make the red-wine reduction, melt 15 g of the butter in a small heavy-based saucepan over medium heat. Add the onion and cook for 3 minutes or until soft but not coloured. Add the wine, stock and sugar and bring to the boil, then reduce the heat to low and simmer for 1 hour or until reduced to one-third; you should have about 1 cup (250 ml). Remove from the heat, cover and set aside in a warm place for 5 minutes, then whisk in the remaining butter. Set aside until needed.

To make the mushrooms, combine the butter and oil in a heavy-based frying pan over high heat. When the butter has melted, add the garlic and cook for 1 minute. Add the mushrooms and salt to taste and cook for another 1–2 minutes or until lightly coloured. Toss the parsley through the mushrooms, then drain in a sieve over a bowl, reserving the liquid and mushrooms separately and discarding the garlic.

Place the stock in a heavy-based saucepan over high heat and bring to a simmer, then reduce the heat to low and cover to keep warm.

Melt 25 g of the unsalted butter in deep heavy-based frying pan over medium heat. Add the rice and a pinch of salt and cook, stirring constantly, for 2–3 minutes or until very hot but not coloured; it should start to smell toasty. Add enough stock to just cover the rice and cook for 8 minutes, adding more stock, a ladle at a time as each ladleful is absorbed, shaking the pan to combine; do not stir. Add the reserved mushroom liquid and start stirring. Cook for another 7–9 minutes or until the rice is al dente, adding more stock as needed and stirring constantly. Remove the pan from the heat, cover and set aside for 1 minute.

Add the acid butter, remaining unsalted butter, Grana and a drizzle of oil and, using a wooden spoon and shaking the pan, beat to create a creamy consistency, adding a little more stock if necessary to get the right consistency.

Spoon onto plates and tap each plate gently on a tea towel-covered workbench to flatten out the risotto. Arrange the mushrooms on top, drizzle with the red-wine reduction and serve.

ISOTTO CON I FEGATINI

RISOTTO WITH CHICKEN LIVERS

We always had chickens in the backyard at home and my *nonna* was the one who killed them. When I was about 13, she taught me how to do it – and I have to say, it was a bit scary. Once they were dead, the first thing she did was take all the guts out, separating the heart, liver, and kidneys. I remember that we handled these parts, in particular the liver, while still warm, which was also a bit disconcerting, but the vibrant flavour you get when they're this fresh isn't achievable any other way – I've always remembered it. Chicken livers prepared like this can also be served as antipasti on crostini.

Serves 6

350 g chicken livers

2 litres Chicken Stock
 (see page 222)

75 g unsalted butter

450 g (about 2¼ cups) carnaroli
 rice (see page 225)

salt flakes

24 sage leaves

¼ cup (60 ml) dry white wine

75g cold Acid Butter (see
 page 224)

50 g Grana Padano, freshly grated

Remove any fat and membrane from the livers and soak them in a bowl of cold water for 30 minutes. Drain and pat dry.

Place the stock in a heavy-based saucepan over high heat and bring to a simmer, then reduce the heat to low and cover.

Melt 50 g of the butter in a deep heavy-based frying pan over medium heat. Add the rice and a pinch of salt and cook, stirring constantly, for 2–3 minutes or until very hot but not coloured; it should start to smell toasty. Add enough stock to just cover the rice and cook for 8 minutes, adding more stock, a ladle at a time as each ladleful is absorbed, shaking the pan to combine; do not stir. Add another ladle of stock and start stirring. Cook for another 7–9 minutes or until the rice is al dente, adding more stock as needed and stirring constantly. Remove the pan from the heat, cover and set aside while cooking the chicken livers.

Melt the remaining butter in a heavy-based frying pan over high heat. Add the livers and cook for 30 seconds, then add the sage and cook for another 30 seconds or until the livers are just coloured all over. Remove the livers and drain on paper towel. Add the wine to the pan and stir to remove any bits stuck to the bottom, then cook for another 2 minutes or so.

Add the acid butter and Grana to the risotto and, using a wooden spoon and shaking the pan, beat to create a creamy consistency, adding a little more stock if necessary to get the right consistency.

Spoon onto plates and tap each plate gently on a tea towel-covered workbench to flatten out the risotto. Arrange the chicken livers and sage leaves on top of the risotto, drizzle with the pan juices and serve.

ISOTTO CON PESCE PERSICO

RISOTTO WITH PERCH FILLETS

Every year my family travelled to Lake Idro to a particular restaurant to eat this risotto during the short season when lake perch is around. It was something we looked forward to all year, and this recipe is a signature dish of the restaurants along the shores of Lombardy's most famous lakes, Lake Idro and Lake Como. Whiting or flathead fillets would also work beautifully in this recipe.

Serves 6

2 litres Fish Stock (see page 221)

175 g unsalted butter

450 g (about 2¼ cups) carnaroli rice (see page 225)

salt flakes

400 g (about 2) silver perch fillets, pin-boned, cut into 18 strips

plain flour, for dusting

75 g cold Acid Butter (see page 224)

100 g Grana Padano, freshly grated

24 sage leaves

Place the stock in a heavy-based saucepan over high heat and bring to a simmer, then reduce the heat to low and cover.

Melt 25 g of the butter in a deep heavy-based frying pan over medium heat. Add the rice and a pinch of salt and cook, stirring constantly, for 2–3 minutes or until very hot but not coloured; it should start to smell toasty. Add enough stock to just cover the rice and cook for 8 minutes, adding more stock, a ladle at a time as each ladleful is absorbed, shaking the pan to combine; do not stir.

Meanwhile, dust the fish in flour, shaking off the excess, then place on a plate. Melt the remaining butter in a large heavy-based frying pan over low heat. Turn off the heat as soon as the butter has melted.

Add another ladle of stock to the rice mixture and start stirring. Cook for another 7–9 minutes or until the rice is al dente, adding more stock as needed and stirring constantly. Remove the pan from the heat, cover and set aside for 1 minute.

Add the acid butter and Grana and, using a wooden spoon and shaking the pan, beat to create a creamy consistency, adding a little more stock if necessary to get the right consistency.

Return the pan of melted butter to high heat, add the sage leaves and fish and cook the fish for 30 seconds on one side, then turn over and remove the pan from the heat.

Spoon the risotto onto plates and tap each plate gently on a tea towel-covered workbench to flatten out the risotto. Using a fish slice or spatula, place the fish on top of the risotto, then sprinkle with salt to taste. Return the butter to high heat until it sizzles, then spoon the butter and sage leaves over the fish and serve.

ISO ALLA PITOCCA

CHICKEN RICE

This is a typical rice dish from my province of Brescia. I like to buy a whole chicken, with the head and feet on if possible, and use them in the stock too for extra flavour; you can order one from a specialist poultry supplier, or just use a headless chicken.

Serves 6

1 × 1.5 kg free-range chicken, with giblets reserved

1 carrot, roughly chopped

1 stalk celery, roughly chopped

2 small onions, peeled and halved

3 litres water, as needed

¼ cup (60 ml) grapeseed oil

100 g unsalted butter

450 g (about 2¼ cups) carnaroli rice (see page 225)

salt flakes

150 ml dry white wine

50 g Grana Padano, freshly grated

1 small handful (about ¼ cup) flat-leaf parsley leaves, very finely chopped

extra virgin olive oil, for drizzling

Remove the excess fat and skin from around the chicken's neck and tail and rinse the cavity with cold water to remove any trace of blood. Remove the neck and first two joints of the wings (leaving the mini-drumsticks attached), and head and feet if using, and set aside with the chicken liver, heart and kidneys from the giblets. Cut the rest of the chicken into 11 pieces (see page 226).

Combine the carrot, celery, one of the onions, the chicken wings, neck, giblets, head and feet (if using) in a large heavy-based saucepan or stockpot. Cover with the water and bring to the boil, then reduce the heat to low and simmer for 2 hours, skimming often to remove any froth that floats to the top. Ladle through a cloth-lined sieve into a clean saucepan discarding the solids, then cover and place over low heat.

Finely chop the remaining onion.

Heat the grapeseed oil in a heavy-based frying pan over medium–high heat, add the chicken pieces and cook for 12 minutes or until well coloured all over. Remove from the pan and set aside. Add the liver, heart and kidneys to the pan and cook, stirring, for 2 minutes or until coloured all over. Set aside. Remove the meat from the chicken pieces, then shred into bite-sized pieces. Discard the bones.

Melt 50 g of the butter in a deep heavy-based frying pan over medium heat. Add the chopped onion and cook for 2–3 minutes or until soft but not coloured. Add the rice and a pinch of salt and cook, stirring constantly, for 2–3 minutes or until very hot but not coloured; it should start to smell toasty. Add the wine and cook for 1–2 minutes or until most of it has evaporated, then add enough stock to just cover the rice and cook for 8 minutes, adding more stock, a ladle at a time as each ladleful is absorbed, shaking the pan to combine; do not stir. Add the chicken meat, heart and kidneys, reserving the liver, and start stirring. Cook for another 7–9 minutes or until the rice is al dente, adding more stock as needed and stirring constantly. Remove the pan from the heat, cover and set aside for 1 minute. Stir in the Grana, parsley and remaining butter.

Spoon the rice mixture into shallow bowls, evenly top with the liver, drizzle with olive oil and serve.

69

RISO ALLA PILOTA

RICE WITH PORK SAUSAGE

Unusually for Lombardy, this traditional dish is always made with vialone nano rice instead of carnaroli – I have no idea why, it just is. I'm also not sure why the rice has to protrude from the water, but every recipe I've ever seen for this dish says it should, so I guess it's important. Perhaps it was a way the *nonnas* had of ensuring the ratio of rice to water was correct – sometimes we just have to trust traditional wisdom. Occasionally roasted pork ribs are added to this dish to make a hearty one-pot meal that I enjoy, then it becomes *riso alla pilota col puntel*.

Serves 4

2 litres Chicken Stock
  (see page 222)

salt flakes

400 g (about 2 cups) vialone nano
  rice (see page 59)

125 g unsalted butter

560 g Italian pork sausage meat
  (see page 225)

24 sage leaves

70 g Grana Padano, freshly grated

Place the stock and salt in a large heavy-based saucepan and bring to the boil. Pour the rice onto a large sheet of baking paper, then carefully lift up the paper and use it as a funnel to pour the rice into the centre of the saucepan so that it forms a mound with the tip protruding about 1 cm above the stock. If the rice is fully covered, carefully remove some of the stock with a ladle until a 1 cm tip of rice is showing. Return to the boil and shake the pan so that the rice is fully submerged. Reduce the heat to low, cover and simmer for 12 minutes, shaking the pan occasionally, then remove from the heat. Set aside with a tea towel wrapped around the saucepan to keep it warm.

While the rice is resting, melt 70 g of the butter in a heavy-based frying pan over high heat. Add the sausage meat and cook, stirring well with a fork to break it up, for 10 minutes or until cooked through.

Meanwhile, heat the remaining butter in a heavy-based frying pan over high heat for 5 minutes or until it starts frothing. Add the sage and cook for 1–2 minutes or until the butter is light brown and the sage is crisp. Remove the pan from the heat.

Add the sausage meat and Grana to the rice and stir well to combine.

Spoon the rice into bowls, pour the sage and butter mixture evenly on top and serve.

GNOCCHI
AND
PASTA

In Lombardy, we don't traditionally grow hard durum wheat for dried pasta, so we make fresh pasta. We love filled pasta too, and never tire of simple burnt butter and sage sauce – it's so delicious, why would you? We also make dumplings (gnocchi) from potatoes or other starchy ingredients like chestnut flour and pumpkin. Pasta and gnocchi are always entrées, and it's important that there is just enough sauce to coat them, not drown them.

GNOCCHI CON ANGUILLA AFFUMICATA E ZUCCHINE

POTATO GNOCCHI WITH SMOKED EEL AND ZUCCHINI

I love how this dish celebrates two typical Lombardian ingredients – eel and gnocchi. I ramp up the flavour by using smoked eel (available from harrissmokehouse.com.au), which works really well with mint, another popular ingredient in Lombardy.

Serves 6

1 × 450 g smoked eel

3 zucchinis (courgettes)

100 ml extra virgin olive oil, plus extra for drizzling

1 clove garlic, thinly sliced

2 golden shallots, thinly sliced

50 ml dry white wine

pinch of saffron threads

⅔ cup (160 ml) Fish Stock (see page 221)

25 g unsalted butter

50 g Grana Padano, freshly grated

6 mint leaves, very thinly sliced

Gnocchi dough

560 g russet or other floury potatoes, scrubbed

rock salt, as needed

80 g cornflour, sifted, plus extra for dusting

50 g Grana Padano, freshly grated

1 teaspoon fine salt

1 pinch of freshly grated nutmeg

1 egg yolk

Remove the skin from the eel, including the thin, dark membrane just under the skin. Pick the meat off the bones and cut into 5 mm dice.

Cut the skin off the zucchinis, leaving about 5 mm flesh on it and discarding the rest. Cut the skin into 5 mm dice.

To make the gnocchi dough, preheat the oven to 180°C.

Place the potatoes on a bed of rock salt on a baking tray and bake for 1–1½ hours or until a wooden skewer can be inserted into a potato without any resistance. Remove the potatoes from the oven, cut in half and immediately press, flesh-side down, through a potato ricer, onto a clean, dry workbench lightly dusted with extra cornflour, spreading it out on the bench. Leave to cool for a few minutes.

Sprinkle the 80 g cornflour, the Grana, fine salt and nutmeg over the potato and place the egg yolk in the centre. Using a pastry scraper and your hands, work the mixture until the dough just comes together; don't overwork it, add a little more cornflour if it's too moist. Shape the dough into a 4 cm-high brick and cut lengthways into 1 cm-thick slices. Cut each slice into 1 cm-thick strips and roll gently with your hands to make them round. Cut the strips into 1 cm-thick pieces.

Bring a large heavy-based saucepan of salted water to the boil, cover and keep it boiling.

Meanwhile, place 50 ml of the oil in a large heavy-based frying pan over medium heat, add the garlic and shallot and cook for 1 minute. Add the zucchini and cook for another 2–3 minutes or until lightly coloured. Pour in the wine and stir well to remove any cooked bits stuck to the bottom of the pan. Add the saffron and stock and bring to a simmer.

Add the gnocchi to the pan of boiling water and cook for 1–2 minutes or until they rise to the surface. Stir the eel through the sauce. As the gnocchi rise, scoop them up with a slotted spoon, drain well and add to the sauce. Gently toss through the sauce, adding the remaining oil, butter and Grana.

Scatter the mint over the top, drizzle with extra oil and serve.

MALFATTI

RICOTTA AND SPINACH GNOCCHI

These delicious gnocchi are found all over Lombardy. The name means 'badly made' because they were originally made from leftover ravioli filling. When cooks ran out of pasta but still had some filling left, they added eggs and flour and made gnocchi with it; these are called *gnuddi* in some regions, meaning 'naked' as they are missing their pasta covering. It's really important to take the butter to a dark-brown stage so it tastes nutty, not greasy – so be brave and keep it on the heat longer than you think you need to.

Serves 6

600 g baby spinach

salt flakes

150 g unsalted butter

1 small onion, finely chopped

1 cup (200 g) well drained fresh
   ricotta (see page 226)

1⅓ cups (200 g) 00 flour
   (see page 225), sifted

2 eggs, lightly beaten

120 g Grana Padano,
   freshly grated

1 pinch of freshly grated nutmeg

freshly ground black pepper

Blanch the spinach, in batches, in a saucepan of boiling salted water for 3 minutes. Place in iced water to cool, then squeeze in a clean tea towel to remove as much excess water as possible and chop it finely.

Melt 75 g of the butter in a heavy-based frying pan over medium heat. Add the onion and cook for 4 minutes or until tender. Add the spinach and cook, stirring often, for 3 minutes. Spread the spinach mixture on a plate to cool. Transfer to a bowl, then add the ricotta, flour, egg, 60 g of the Grana, the nutmeg and salt and pepper to taste. Mix gently to form a dough. Cover and refrigerate for at least 30 minutes to firm, this helps the gnocchi hold together during cooking.

Bring a large heavy-based saucepan of salted water to the boil.

Working in batches and using 2 wet dessertspoons, scoop up a spoonful of mixture and use the second spoon to slide it into the water. Cook for 1–2 minutes or until they rise to the surface. As they rise, scoop them up with a slotted spoon, drain well and place on a platter.

Meanwhile, melt the remaining butter in a small heavy-based saucepan over high heat and cook until it turns dark nut-brown.

Sprinkle the remaining Grana over the gnocchi, pour the brown butter over the top and serve.

GNOCCHI DI ZUCCA AL GORGONZOLA

PUMPKIN GNOCCHI WITH GORGONZOLA SAUCE

One of my cousins married a Mantuan, and I remember looking forward to visiting them in Mantua as we always got to enjoy their different regional specialities, even though they only lived 45 minutes away. This style of gnocchi is traditional to Mantua, as they grow a lot of pumpkins. Their pumpkins are a lot drier and more floury than Australian ones. In Australia, the type of pumpkin available often depends on the season, and the moisture content varies a lot between different types, and even from pumpkin to pumpkin, depending on how long they've been stored. Sometimes, if there's a lot of moisture in the purée, I wrap it in muslin and hang it over a bowl in the restaurant cool room to drain for a while.

Serves 8

1 kg russet or other floury
   potatoes, scrubbed

2.2 kg butternut pumpkin
   (squash), cut into eighths and
   seeds removed

rock salt, as needed

1⅔ cups (250 g) plain flour, plus
   extra for dusting

250 g cornflour, plus extra
   if needed

250 g Grana Padano,
   freshly grated

fine salt

2 eggs

1 cup (250 ml) water

100 g unsalted butter

24 sage leaves

300 g gorgonzola dolce, diced

Preheat the oven to 180°C.

Place the potatoes and pumpkin on a bed of rock salt on a baking tray and bake for 1–1½ hours or until a wooden skewer can be inserted into a potato without any resistance. Remove from the oven, cut the potatoes in half and immediately press, flesh-side down, through a potato ricer, onto a clean, dry workbench lightly dusted with extra flour, spreading it out on the bench. Remove the pumpkin skin and press the flesh through the ricer onto the potato. Leave to cool for a few minutes.

Sift the combined plain flour and cornflour over the top, sprinkle with 200 g of the Grana and fine salt to taste and break the eggs into the centre. Using a pastry scraper and your hands, work the mixture until the dough just comes together; don't overwork it, add a little more cornflour if it's too moist.

Shape the dough into a 4 cm-high brick, cut lengthways into 1 cm-thick slices. Cut each slice into 1 cm-thick strips and roll gently with your hands to form logs. Cut the logs into 1 cm-thick pieces.

Bring a large heavy-based saucepan of salted water to the boil. Add the gnocchi and cook for 1–2 minutes or until they rise to the surface.

Meanwhile, combine the water, butter and sage leaves in a heavy-based frying pan over medium heat. As the gnocchi rise to the surface, scoop them up with a slotted spoon, drain well and add to the frying pan. Gently toss for a couple of minutes to coat well.

Remove from the heat, add the gorgonzola and remaining Grana and continue tossing until the cheese has melted. Transfer to a platter or divide among plates and serve.

GNOCCHI DI CASTAGNE AL BURRO E SALVIA

CHESTNUT GNOCCHI WITH BUTTER AND SAGE

Chestnut trees grow wild in the woods of Lombardy and in autumn, when chestnuts are in season, families including mine rummage through the woods collecting them. We roast some, use some as a pasta filling (see page 97), some go into desserts and the rest are dried and ground into flour, then used in dishes like this. Chestnut woods produce the best porcini mushrooms too, so we gather them and the chestnuts at the same time. This dish can be gluten-free if you use corn-based cornflour.

Serves 6

1.2 kg russet or other floury
    potatoes, scrubbed

rock salt, as needed

½ cup (75 g) cornflour,
    sifted, plus extra for
    dusting and if needed

½ cup (75 g) chestnut flour
    (see page 225), sifted

150 g Grana Padano,
    freshly grated

1 pinch of freshly grated nutmeg

salt flakes

2 egg yolks

Butter and sage sauce

150 g unsalted butter

1 clove garlic, bruised

5 sage leaves

Preheat the oven to 180°C.

Place the potatoes on a bed of rock salt on a baking tray and bake for 1–1½ hours or until a wooden skewer can be inserted into a potato without any resistance. Remove from the oven, cut in half and immediately press, flesh-side down, through a potato ricer, onto a clean, dry workbench lightly dusted with extra cornflour, spreading it out on the bench. Leave to cool for a few minutes.

Sprinkle the cornflour, chestnut flour, 75 g of the Grana, the nutmeg and salt to taste over the top and place the egg yolks in the centre. Using a pastry scraper and your hands, work the mixture until the dough just comes together; don't overwork it, add a little more cornflour if it's too moist.

Shape the dough into a 5 cm-high brick, cut lengthways into 2 cm-thick slices, cut each slice into 2 cm-thick strips and roll gently with your hands to form logs. Cut the logs into 2 cm-thick pieces.

Bring a large heavy-based saucepan of salted water to the boil and keep it boiling.

To make the butter and sage sauce, place the butter and garlic in a large heavy-based frying pan over low heat. As soon as the butter melts, add the sage leaves to the pan and the gnocchi to the boiling water. Cook the gnocchi for 1–2 minutes or until they rise to the surface. As they rise, scoop them up with a slotted spoon, drain well and add to the butter sauce.

Gently toss the gnocchi through the butter and sage sauce, adding the remaining Grana. Remove and discard the garlic and serve.

GNOCCHI DI ORTICHE CON POMODORO

NETTLE GNOCCHI WITH TOMATO SAUCE

When we harvest nettles from the wild in Italy, we only pick the young shoots and tops, as they are the most tender. If nettles aren't available, use spinach, silverbeet or another leafy green.

Serves 4

100 g nettles, prepared (see page 226)

salt flakes

420 g russet or other floury potatoes, scrubbed

rock salt, as needed

90 g cornflour, sifted, plus extra for dusting and if needed

40 g Grana Padano, freshly grated

1 pinch of freshly grated nutmeg

fine salt

1 egg yolk

Tomato sauce

50 ml extra virgin olive oil

1 clove garlic, chopped

1 golden shallot, chopped

1 small oxheart tomato or large vine-ripened tomato, diced

16 basil leaves

Bring a large heavy-based saucepan of salted water to the boil. Add the nettles and boil for 5 minutes, then place in iced water to cool. Drain well, squeezing to remove as much moisture as possible; once they're cooked they no longer sting. Transfer to a food processor and process for 5 minutes or until a very smooth purée forms, adding a little water if necessary to help it blend. Transfer to a small heavy-based saucepan and cook over medium heat for 15–30 minutes or until it's quite thick and most of the water has evaporated.

Preheat the oven to 180°C.

Place the potatoes on a bed of rock salt on a baking tray and bake for 1–1½ hours or until a wooden skewer can be inserted into a potato without any resistance.

Meanwhile, to make the tomato sauce, heat the oil in a large heavy-based frying pan over medium heat. Add the garlic and shallot and cook for 1 minute. Add the tomato and cook for 2–3 minutes or until pulpy. Stir in the basil, reduce the heat to low and cook for another 10 minutes or until slightly thickened. Remove from the heat and set aside.

Remove the potatoes from the oven, cut in half and immediately press, flesh-side down, through a potato ricer, onto a clean, dry workbench lightly dusted with extra cornflour, spreading it out on the bench. Leave to cool for a few minutes.

Sprinkle the cornflour, 20 g of the Grana, nutmeg and fine salt to taste over the top and place the egg yolk and nettle purée in the centre. Using a pastry scraper and your hands, work the mixture until the dough just comes together; don't overwork it, add a little more cornflour if it's too moist. Shape the dough into a 4 cm-high brick, then cut lengthways into 2 cm-thick slices. Cut each slice into 2 cm-thick strips and roll gently with your hands to form logs. Cut the logs into 2 cm-thick pieces.

Reheat the sauce over medium heat.

Bring a large heavy-based saucepan of salted water to the boil. Add the gnocchi and cook for 1–2 minutes or until they rise to the surface. Scoop them up with a slotted spoon, drain well and add to the sauce.

Gently toss through the sauce, adding the remaining Grana. Serve on a platter or divide among bowls.

GNOCCHI

Common in northern European cooking, dumplings are also typical of Lombardy – we call them gnocchi, or gnocchetti if they are small.

The secrets to deliciously light gnocchi are touching the dough as little as possible and using a minimum amount of flour.

A potato ricer (see page 227), which looks like a giant garlic crusher, is an inexpensive investment that gives the best results. As you don't have to peel the potatoes, you can push them through the ricer while they're still too hot to handle. You could pass them through a mouli or a fine-mesh sieve, but a ricer gives the lightest texture.

You want to use just enough flour to hold the dough together, so start with less then, before shaping the gnocchi, break off a small piece of dough and cook it to check that it holds together. If it doesn't, mix in just a little more flour and check again. I often mix some cornflour with the wheaten flour, as it's lighter and absorbs moisture well without going gluey. I've even made gluten-free gnocchi using just maize cornflour or rice flour without any wheaten flour.

A wooden bench is the best surface to make gnocchi on, as it absorbs excess moisture, making the dough as dry as possible with less flour. The type of potato helps with this too – I prefer russet, but desiree, spunta and other floury potatoes are also good. As low moisture content is what's most important, some waxy potatoes, including kipflers, also work well.

Ideally, you'll cook, sauce and eat the gnocchi immediately. However, if you need to plan ahead, they can be cooked, cooled in iced water, drained well, tossed with a little olive oil, spread on a tray, covered with plastic film and refrigerated for up to two days. When you're ready to serve them, add them to a large pan of boiling water and scoop them out as soon as they float to the surface.

I love leftover gnocchi spread in a buttered baking dish, topped with a little extra grated Grana and baked at 200°C for 30 minutes until they're really well coloured and slightly crisp.

PASTA

I like to make the dough for fresh pasta quite dry because when you rest it, the dough softens a little anyway – if it feels the right texture at first it will be too soft by the time it has rested. This means it can be difficult to mix by hand, so use a food processor if you prefer. You can also use an electric mixer fitted with a dough hook, which is easier than kneading by hand. Some pasta machines also come with a kneading attachment.

A hand-operated pasta machine, available from kitchenware stores, is essential for making good fresh pasta. Some people say you need to pass the dough through the machine many times with lots of folding and turning, but I don't like to overwork the dough, so I only pass it a few times, reducing the thickness setting a couple of notches each time. For long pasta like tagliatelle I pass the dough a total of four times, while for filled pasta, where you have a double thickness of dough around the edges, a total of six times.

If you shape the dough into a neat rectangle before you start passing it through the machine, you'll have very little wastage. Once I've cut the pasta into shapes, I don't like to pass the offcuts back through the machine, as the reworked dough is never as delicate. Instead, I cut the offcuts into rough strips, called *stracci* (meaning 'rags'), to make a quick pasta for staff dinner, but you could repass the dough if you like.

The cut pasta can be left for a few hours on a semolina-covered tray. Be generous with the semolina as it stops the pasta from sticking together: I use about half a 375 g packet of fine semolina for a 60 cm × 40 cm tray and toss the pasta through it as I put it onto the tray. When I'm making filled pasta, I spray it lightly using a spray gun of water on the mist setting, to help the pasta seal around the filling.

Use plenty of salted water brought to a rolling boil in a large saucepan to cook pasta – at least 4 litres water for every 500 g pasta with 10 g salt per litre. Fresh pasta cooks a lot quicker than dried pasta (as it contains a lot more moisture), taking only 2–3 minutes to float to the surface of the water, the sign that it's ready. And, unlike dried pasta, it doesn't cook to a firm 'al dente' bite, but is tender with just a little resistance to the tooth. Once the pasta is cooked, act quickly: drain it in a large colander (reserving some cooking water to add to the sauce if needed), toss it through the sauce and serve immediately in heated bowls.

PASTA FRESCA

FRESH PASTA DOUGH

If you want to make a smaller quantity, use 100 g flour per egg for each 150 g pasta dough. This quantity of dough will make about eight serves.

Makes about 750 g

3⅓ cups (500 g) 00 flour (see page 225), plus extra for dusting

5 × 60 g eggs

Sift the flour into a large bowl, break the eggs on top and mix in with a fork.

Using your hands, bring the mixture together to form a firm dough. Tip onto a clean, dry workbench lightly dusted with extra flour and knead the dough for 5 minutes or until smooth; dust your hands or the bench with a little more flour if the dough starts to stick. Wrap in plastic film and refrigerate for at least 30 minutes.

Cut the dough into six pieces and flatten one piece slightly into a neat rectangle, wrapping the remaining pieces in plastic film to prevent them drying out.

Starting on the widest setting, pass the flattened piece of dough through a pasta machine the necessary number of times, depending on the recipe, reducing the setting by 2 notches each time (see page 85).

Dust the dough lightly with flour if it starts to stick; if it becomes too long to handle, cut it in half, dust the half you aren't working on lightly with flour and continue with each half separately. Repeat with the remaining dough.

Cook as specified in the recipe.

TAGLIATELLE CON IL PASTÖM

TAGLIATELLE WITH FRESH SALAMI SAUCE

Pastöm is a dialect word for the mixture that salami is made from; if you can, ask a butcher who makes his own salami to sell you the filling without the casings, or buy fresh (not cured) salami and peel the skins off. When I was 19, I worked for the butcher in our hometown and, when we'd finish salami making for the day, we made patties from the leftover *pastöm*, then cooked them on an open fire for a snack. This rich sauce is also great with the bigoli on page 94.

Serves 6

2 tablespoons extra virgin olive oil

50 g unsalted butter

1 onion, finely diced

2 stalks pale inner celery heart, finely diced

1 carrot, finely diced

2 small dried red chillies, chopped

400 g fresh salami mixture (see recipe introduction)

⅓ cup (80 ml) dry white wine

1 cup (260 g) tomato passata

2 fresh bay leaves

fine salt

500 g Fresh Pasta Dough (see page 86), passed through the pasta machine 4 times

fine semolina, for dusting

50 g Grana Padano, freshly grated

Heat the oil and butter in a heavy-based frying pan over medium heat until the butter melts. Add the onion, celery, carrot and chilli and cook for 3 minutes or until lightly coloured. Crumble the salami mixture into the pan and cook, stirring often, for 2–3 minutes or until well coloured. Add the wine and cook for 1 minute or until it evaporates. Add the passata and bay leaves and bring to the boil, then reduce the heat to low and simmer, covered, for 15 minutes, stirring occasionally. Add salt to taste, then cover and keep warm over the lowest heat.

Meanwhile, lay one sheet of the pasta dough on a clean, dry workbench lightly dusted with semolina, then dust the dough with more semolina. Cut the sheet into three 25 cm-long strips and stack them on top of each other, with semolina dusted in between. Fold the stack in half and slice lengthways into 1 cm-wide strips. Place on a semolina-dusted tray and repeat with the remaining sheets.

Bring a large heavy-based saucepan of salted water to the boil. Add the pasta and cook for 2 minutes or until tender. Using tongs, lift the pasta out of the water and add to the sauce. Add the Grana and toss well to coat, adding a little of the pasta cooking water if necessary to give a creamy consistency. Serve in shallow pasta bowls or on plates.

PAPPARDELLE AL CINGHIALE

PAPPARDELLE WITH ELSA'S WILD BOAR RAGÙ

Wild boars are now regarded as pests in the woods of Lombardy because they have such large litters. To counter this, the government encourages hunting by extending the season, and hunters can take as many boars as they want. My parents' best friends, Elsa and her husband, Tulio, have a hunting lodge in the mountains and Tulio is a keen hunter. Ever since I was young we visited them there and looked forward to Elsa's pasta or polenta with wild boar. The boar is always freshly caught and hung for a few days before cooking. On the way there I'd be hungry in anticipation of this dish. Still today, when I take people up there, Elsa always serves this. Vic's Meat in Sydney sell wild boar online and will airfreight orders to anywhere in Australia: vicsmeat.com.au.

Serves 6

50 ml grapeseed oil

2 white onions, sliced

500 g wild boar shoulder meat, cut into 3 cm cubes

2½ tablespoons grappa (see page 225)

6 juniper berries

2 fresh bay leaves

salt flakes

3 cups (750 ml) red wine, as needed to cover

1 cup (250 ml) Chicken Stock (see page 222)

500 g Fresh Pasta Dough (see page 86), passed through the pasta machine 4 times

fine semolina, for dusting

100 g unsalted butter

60 g Grana Padano, freshly grated

1 small handful (about ¼ cup) flat-leaf parsley leaves, very finely chopped

Heat the oil in a heavy-based saucepan over medium heat. Add the onion and cook for 10 minutes or until lightly coloured. Increase the heat to high and add the meat. Cook for 6 minutes, turning to colour all sides. Add the grappa, juniper berries, bay leaves and salt to taste and cook for 2–3 minutes or until the grappa has evaporated. Add enough wine to cover the meat and return to the boil, then reduce the heat to low. Simmer, covered, and stirring occasionally, for 2 hours; the meat should be falling apart. Remove the meat and chop it finely, then return to the pan. Add the stock and bring it to the boil, then remove the pan from the heat, cover and set aside for 30 minutes to rest.

Meanwhile, lay one sheet of the pasta dough on a clean, dry workbench lightly dusted with semolina and dust the dough with more semolina. Cut the sheet into three 25 cm-long strips and stack them on top of each other with semolina dusted in between. Fold the stack in half and slice lengthways into 2 cm-wide strips. Place on a semolina-dusted tray and repeat with the remaining sheets.

Bring a large heavy-based saucepan of salted water to the boil. Add the pasta and cook for 2 minutes or until tender.

Meanwhile, reheat the sauce over low heat.

Using tongs, lift the pasta out of the water, add to the sauce and toss well to coat, adding a little of the pasta cooking water if necessary to give a creamy consistency. Add the butter, Grana and parsley and toss again until the butter melts and is completely incorporated into the sauce. Serve on a platter or divide among plates.

IZZOCCHERI

BUCKWHEAT PASTA WITH POTATO, CABBAGE AND CHEESE

This classic dish from the cold, high valley of Valtellina is delicious, hearty winter fare. Buckwheat doesn't have the gluten of wheat, so be patient as this dough is a lot more crumbly than regular pasta dough. You'll get the best result if you shape the dough into a very neat rectangle before passing it through the pasta machine; if it breaks when you pass it, just reshape it and try again. If you don't have a dough hook attachment for your electric mixer you can knead the dough by hand – but it's very hard work.

Serves 6

salt flakes

1 large desiree potato, peeled and cut into 1 cm dice

200 g Savoy cabbage, shredded

200 g unsalted butter, plus extra for buttering

½ white onion, finely chopped

1 small clove garlic, finely chopped

6 sage leaves, shredded

300 g fontina cheese, cut into 1 cm dice

1 handful (about ½ cup) flat-leaf parsley leaves, finely chopped

50 g Grana Padano, freshly grated

Pizzoccheri dough

2 cups (300 g) buckwheat flour (see page 225)

1⅓ cups (200 g) 00 flour (see page 225), plus extra for dusting

4 × 60 g eggs

fine salt

fine semolina, for dusting

To make the pizzoccheri dough, sift the combined buckwheat and 00 flours into the bowl of an electric mixer fitted with a dough hook, add the eggs and salt to taste and mix for 5 minutes or until a smooth dough forms. If it's too dry to come together, add a teaspoon of water at a time and mix this into the dough until it comes together; don't be tempted to add too much water at a time as the dough can become too wet very quickly. Wrap in plastic film and refrigerate for at least 30 minutes.

Cover the base of a large tray with a thick layer of semolina. Dust a clean, dry workbench with semolina. Cut the dough into six pieces and flatten one piece slightly into a neat rectangle, wrapping the remaining pieces in plastic film to prevent them drying out. Dust the dough with flour and pass it through a pasta machine on the widest setting. Reduce the setting by one notch and pass again. Lay the pasta on the bench and repeat with the remaining dough. Stack two strips of dough on top of each other and, with a sharp knife, cut into 3 mm-wide lengths. Place on the prepared tray, tossing them in the semolina, and repeat with the remaining dough.

Preheat the oven to 220°C.

Bring a large heavy-based saucepan of salted water to the boil. Add the potato and boil for 3 minutes. Add the cabbage and return to the boil. Add the pasta and boil for 6 minutes or until the pasta is tender. Drain and place in a buttered baking dish large enough to fit all the ingredients.

Meanwhile, melt the butter in a heavy-based frying pan over medium heat. Add the onion, garlic and a pinch of salt and cook for 3 minutes or until soft but not coloured. Add the sage leaves and cook over high heat until the butter turns dark nut-brown.

Add the fontina and parsley to the pasta mixture and toss well to combine. Scatter the Grana over the top, then pour the butter mixture over and bake for 15 minutes. Serve straight from the baking dish.

IGOLI CON LE SARDELLE

BIGOLI WITH SARDINES

Bigoli is like thick spaghetti – it's made using a special device called a *torchio*, a hand-cranked extruder. Duck eggs are traditionally used in the dough, but as most people don't have an extruder (or easy access to duck eggs), I've developed this eggless dough that's not as firm and crumbly, so it's easier to roll by hand. The toasted breadcrumbs aren't traditional, but I think they really lift this dish to another level.

Serves 8

100 ml extra virgin olive oil, plus extra for drizzling

50 g unsalted butter

1 white onion, finely chopped

salt flakes

24 sardine fillets, skin on, pin-boned

1½ tablespoons dry white wine

1 handful (about ½ cup) flat-leaf parsley leaves, finely chopped

1 lemon

Bigoli dough

1⅔ cups (250 g) 00 flour (see page 225), sifted

125 g wholemeal plain flour, sifted

100 g fine semolina, sifted

1½ tablespoons dry white wine

1 cup (250 ml) water, as needed

fine semolina, for dusting

Toasted lemon breadcrumbs

50 g unsalted butter

1 cup (70 g) fine fresh breadcrumbs (see page 226)

1 clove garlic, bruised

finely grated zest of 1 lemon

salt flakes

To make the bigoli dough, place the flours and semolina in the bowl of an electric mixer fitted with a dough hook. With the motor running, add the wine, then gradually add only enough of the water to form a firm dough; you may not need it all. Wrap in plastic film and refrigerate for at least 30 minutes.

Cut the dough into six pieces and flatten one piece slightly into a neat rectangle, wrapping the remaining pieces in plastic film to prevent them drying out. Pass the dough through a pasta machine on the widest setting. Lay the sheet out on a clean, dry workbench lightly dusted with semolina and cut along the short edge into 5 mm-wide strips. Roll each strip with your hands into a long thick strand. Place on a tray, dust lightly with semolina, cover with plastic film and set aside. Repeat with the remaining dough.

Heat the oil and butter in a heavy-based frying pan over low heat. Add the onion and a pinch of salt and cook, covered, for 15–20 minutes or until very soft but not coloured; if the onion starts to colour, add a little warm water.

Meanwhile, to make the toasted breadcrumbs, melt the butter in a small heavy-based frying pan. Add the breadcrumbs and garlic and stir over medium heat for a few minutes until the breadcrumbs turn golden. Remove from the heat, stir in the lemon zest and salt to taste and set aside.

Add the sardines to the onion mixture, increase the heat to high and cook for 5 minutes or until the sardines have almost dissolved, stirring well to break them up. Stir in the wine.

Meanwhile, bring a large heavy-based saucepan of salted water to the boil, add the pasta and cook for 4 minutes or until tender. Using tongs, lift the pasta out of the water and add to the sauce. Add the parsley and a drizzle of oil and toss well to coat, adding a little of the pasta cooking water if necessary to give the sauce a creamy consistency.

Divide among shallow pasta bowls and sprinkle with the toasted breadcrumbs (discarding the bruised garlic). Finely grate over some lemon zest, drizzle with more oil and serve.

ORTELLI DI CASTAGNE

CHESTNUT TORTELLI WITH SAUSAGE AND THYME

When we were kids, every Sunday my brother, Nicola, wanted *Mamma* to make this dish for him, whether chestnuts were in season or not.

Serves 8

300 g Italian pork sausage meat (see page 225)

2 teaspoons extra virgin olive oil

50 g unsalted butter

¼ cup (60 ml) water

3 sprigs thyme, leaves picked

Chestnut tortelli

500 g chestnuts

1.5 litres water

1 fresh bay leaf

10 g rock salt

2 eggs, lightly beaten

100 g Grana Padano, freshly grated

fine semolina, for dusting

300 g Fresh Pasta Dough (see page 86), passed through the pasta machine 6 times

salt flakes

To start making the tortelli, using a sharp knife, slit the chestnut shells. Place the chestnuts in a large heavy-based saucepan with the water, bay leaf and rock salt and bring to the boil. Reduce the heat to low and simmer, covered, for 50 minutes or until a wooden skewer inserted through the slits passes easily into the chestnuts. Drain and set aside until cool enough to handle. Remove the shells and the brown skin coating the chestnuts.

Meanwhile, shape the sausage meat into 1 cm balls, place on a plate, cover and refrigerate until needed.

Press the chestnuts through a drum sieve (see page 227) into a bowl. Add the egg and Grana and stir well to make a smooth mixture. Refrigerate for at least 30 minutes, then roll into ½ teaspoon balls.

Cover the base of a large tray with a thick layer of semolina. Lay the pasta sheets on a clean, dry workbench lightly dusted with semolina and, using an 8.5 cm round cutter, cut into discs. Place a ball of chestnut filling in the centre of each disc and, using a spray bottle, mist very lightly with water. Leaving the parcels on the workbench, fold each in half to enclose, pressing around the filling to remove as much air as possible. Hold the two flaps either side of the filling, then use your thumbs to push the centre of the base away from you, which draws the two corners together to form a rounded shape, wrapping the two corners around your index finger and pressing to stick them together. Place in a single layer on the tray and set aside in a cool place until needed.

Heat the oil in a heavy-based frying pan over high heat. Add the sausage balls and cook for 2–3 minutes or until well coloured on all sides and cooked through. Set aside on paper towel to drain.

Bring a large heavy-based saucepan of salted water to the boil, add the tortelli and cook for 4 minutes or until they rise to the surface and are tender around the edges.

Meanwhile, place the butter in a clean heavy-based frying pan over medium heat. Add the water and whisk to form an emulsion. As the tortelli rise to the surface, scoop them up with a slotted spoon, drain well and add to the butter mixture. Add the sausage balls and thyme and swirl the pan gently to combine.

Serve immediately in shallow pasta bowls.

GNOLOTTI DI PESCE

SNAPPER AGNOLOTTI WITH TOMATO AND OREGANO SAUCE

Here is one of the dishes I loved making at the first restaurant I ever worked in, Fior di Roccia on Lake Garda. Decades later, the chef, Renato, is still my good friend and I always think of him when I make this now. He makes his agnolotti with the carp or freshwater snook found in Lake Garda, but any white-fleshed fish works well. Scissors are the secret for cutting the pasta to get the fold right.

Serves 6

2 × 650 g snapper, gilled, gutted and scaled, with heads and tails discarded

grapeseed oil, for rubbing

2 sprigs fresh bay leaves

½ cup (125 ml) pouring (pure) cream

2 egg whites

1½ tablespoons extra virgin olive oil

fine salt and freshly ground black pepper

80 g Grana Padano, freshly grated

1 small handful chives, chopped

500 g Fresh Pasta Dough (see page 86), passed through the pasta machine 6 times

fine semolina, for dusting

Tomato and oregano sauce

2½ tablespoons extra virgin olive oil

1 golden shallot, finely chopped

salt flakes

2 roma (plum) tomatoes, peeled, seeded and diced

1 tablespoon oregano leaves, plus extra to garnish

freshly ground black pepper

Rub the fish with the grapeseed oil. Place a sprig of bay leaves in a steamer basket, then place the fish on top, followed by the remaining bay leaves. Place over a heavy-based saucepan or wok of boiling water, cover and steam for 15 minutes or until a top fin can easily be pulled loose. Set aside to cool, then pick the flesh off the bones, discarding the skin and bones.

Place the fish flesh in a food processor with the cream, egg whites, olive oil and salt and pepper to taste, then process until smooth. Stir in the Grana and chives. Place in a piping bag and refrigerate.

Working one at a time, cut each sheet of pasta dough in half lengthways and lay both halves on a clean, dry workbench lightly dusted with semolina. Pipe about ½ teaspoon of filling 3.5 cm from the top of one of the pasta halves, in the centre, then continue piping the filling at 7 cm intervals. Fold the pasta half over to cover the filling, pressing lightly to remove the air. Using kitchen scissors and leaving the filled pasta on the workbench, snip between the mounds of filling, halfway through the pasta. Squeeze either side of the filling to extract as much air as possible and press the two 'flaps' forward to seal. Using a pasta wheel, trim off the ends and along the front of the filling to seal, then cut either side of the filling. Place on a tray dusted with semolina, then repeat with the remaining pasta and filling. Set aside.

To make the tomato and oregano sauce, heat the oil in a heavy-based frying pan over medium heat. Add the shallot and salt to taste and cook for 2–3 minutes or until soft but not coloured. Add the tomato and cook for another 5 minutes or until the tomato has broken down. Stir in the oregano and pepper to taste.

Meanwhile, bring a large heavy-based saucepan of salted water to the boil. Add the agnolotti and cook for 4 minutes or until they rise to the surface and are tender around the edges. As they rise, scoop them up with a slotted spoon and drain well, then add to the sauce. Swirl the pan gently to coat.

Serve immediately in shallow pasta bowls, garnished with extra oregano.

ARUBINI

PORK, VEAL AND BEEF RAVIOLI

Marubini filling traditionally includes veal brains, which gives it a lighter texture, but you could leave them out if you prefer. In Mantua, they add fresh ginger, and some people add parsley – I prefer not to.

Serves 8

fine semolina, for dusting

750 g Fresh Pasta Dough (see page 86), passed through the pasta machine 6 times

00 flour (see page 225), for dusting

4 litres Beef Stock (see page 221)

150 g Grana Padano, freshly grated

Pork, veal and beef filling

200 g unsalted butter

1 × 150 g piece beef shoulder meat, diced

1 × 150 g piece veal shoulder meat, diced

1 × 150 g piece pork shoulder meat, diced

2 cups (500 ml) Beef Stock (see page 221)

1 lemon, halved

150 g veal brains

2 egg yolks

75 g Grana Padano, freshly grated

1 tablespoon fine fresh breadcrumbs (see page 226)

1 pinch of freshly grated nutmeg

fine salt

To make the filling, melt the butter in a large heavy-based saucepan over medium heat. Add the beef, veal and pork and increase the heat to high, then cook for 8–10 minutes or until the meat is cooked through and the butter has clarified (the sediment will have settled). Add the stock, and bring to the boil, then reduce the heat to low. Cover and simmer, stirring occasionally, for 35 minutes or until the meat is starting to fall apart. Drain, reserving the liquid and the meat separately.

Meanwhile, bring a heavy-based saucepan of water to the boil and squeeze in juice from half of the lemon, then add the squeezed lemon half to the water. Add the brains, reduce the heat to low and simmer for 5 minutes or until the brains are cooked through. Drain and place the brains in a food processor. Add the meat mixture and process to a coarse paste.

Transfer to a bowl with the egg yolks, Grana, breadcrumbs, nutmeg and salt to taste. Finely grate the zest of the remaining lemon half into the bowl and mix well to form a firm paste. If the mixture is too dry, add just enough of the reserved meat cooking liquid to achieve the right consistency. Transfer to a piping bag.

Cover the base of a large tray with a thick layer of semolina. Working one at a time, cut each sheet of pasta dough in half and lay both halves on a clean, dry workbench lightly dusted with semolina. Pipe about 2 teaspoons of filling 3 cm from the top of one pasta strip, in the centre, then continue piping the filling at 6 cm intervals. Using a spray bottle, mist very lightly with water, then place the other half of the pasta over the top to cover the filling. Sprinkle lightly with flour and gently press around each mound of filling with the back of a 3.5 cm round cutter, rotating the cutter around the filling to push out as much air as possible and pressing firmly to seal. Using a 5 cm round cutter, cut around each mound of filling to form the ravioli. Place on the tray and repeat with the remaining pasta and filling. Press any offcuts of pasta dough into a ball, break into pieces and pass through the pasta machine to form sheets, then repeat until all of the dough and filling have been used. (Makes about 64 ravioli.)

Place the stock in a large heavy-based saucepan and bring to the boil. Add half the ravioli and cook for 4 minutes or until they rise to the surface and are tender around the edges. Divide the ravioli among 8 warm shallow bowls. Repeat with the remaining ravioli.

Ladle some stock over the ravioli, sprinkle with Grana and serve.

CASONCELLI ALLA BRESCIANA

BRESCIAN RAVIOLI WITH BURNT BUTTER AND SAGE

As with so many traditional recipes, *casoncelli* vary from one province to another. There's a particularly fierce debate between the Brescians and the people from Bergamo over whether to include pancetta or not.

Serves 6

2 teaspoons extra virgin olive oil

150 g unsalted butter

1½ tablespoons finely chopped pale inner celery heart

1½ tablespoons finely chopped white onion

1½ tablespoons finely chopped carrot

1 small clove garlic, finely chopped

fine salt

100 g pork neck, diced

100 g veal shoulder, diced

20 g Italian pork sausage meat (see page 225)

20 g mortadella

freshly ground black pepper

100 ml dry white wine

1½ tablespoons finely chopped flat-leaf parsley

1 egg, lightly beaten

1 pinch of freshly grated nutmeg

100 g Grana Padano, freshly grated

28 sage leaves

300 g Fresh Pasta Dough (see page 86), passed through the pasta machine 6 times

fine semolina, for dusting

Combine the oil and 10 g of the butter in a heavy-based saucepan over medium heat. Add the celery, onion, carrot, garlic and salt to taste and cook for 1–2 minutes or until soft but not coloured. Add the pork, veal, sausage meat, mortadella and pepper to taste, and cook for another 8 minutes, stirring occasionally. Add the wine to the pan and stir to remove any bits stuck to the bottom. Bring to the boil, then reduce the heat to low and cook for another 5–7 minutes or until just a little sauce is left.

Set aside to cool to room temperature. Transfer the mixture to a food processor, then pulse until very finely chopped. Place in a bowl and add the parsley, egg, nutmeg and 50 g of the Grana.

Thinly slice 10 of the sage leaves. Heat 30 g of the butter in a small heavy-based frying pan over high heat until light brown. Add the sliced sage and toss for 30 seconds or until crisp, then add to the meat filling. Using your hands, mix well to form a smooth mixture. Cover and refrigerate until needed.

Lay the pasta dough on a clean, dry workbench lightly dusted with semolina and, using an 8 cm round cutter, cut into discs. Place 1 teaspoon of the meat filling in the centre of each disc. Using a spray bottle, mist very lightly with water, then fold in half to enclose, pressing around the filling to remove as much air as possible.

Bring a large heavy-based saucepan of salted water to the boil. Add the *casoncelli* and cook for 4 minutes or until they rise to the surface and are tender around the edges.

Meanwhile, melt the remaining butter in a small heavy-based frying pan over low heat. As the *casoncelli* rise to the surface, scoop them up with a slotted spoon and drain well, then place on a warmed serving platter or divide among plates and sprinkle with the remaining Grana.

Increase the heat under the pan of butter to high and cook until it turns dark nut-brown. Add the remaining sage, toss for 30 seconds or until crisp, then pour over the *casoncelli* and serve.

TORTELLI DI ZUCCA

PUMPKIN TORTELLI

This is a traditional dish from the province of Mantua, featuring the pumpkins that it is renowned for growing on its foggy, humid plains. Mantuans drain the pumpkin in muslin to remove some of the excess moisture and concentrate the flavour, but I find it easier to cook the purée to dry it out. These flavoursome tortelli are always part of the traditional Christmas Eve meal in Mantua. If you can't get apple mustard fruits, use another type.

Serves 6

1.2 kg Queensland blue pumpkin (squash), peeled, seeded and cut into chunks

extra virgin olive oil, for drizzling

20 g amaretti, crushed

50 g apple mustard fruits (see page 225), finely chopped

150 g Grana Padano, freshly grated

1 pinch of freshly grated nutmeg

fine salt and freshly ground black pepper

fine semolina, for dusting

300 g Fresh Pasta Dough (see page 86), passed through the pasta machine 6 times

150 g unsalted butter

1 large handful sage leaves

Preheat the oven to 180°C.

Place the pumpkin on a baking tray lined with baking paper. Drizzle with the oil and bake for 40–60 minutes or until very tender. Set aside to cool a little, then transfer to a food processor and blend until a smooth purée forms.

Place the pumpkin purée in a heavy-based saucepan over medium heat and cook, stirring often, for 30 minutes or until most of the excess moisture has evaporated and the pumpkin is quite dry. Place in a heatproof bowl and set aside to cool. Stir in the amaretti, mustard fruit, 100 g of the Grana, nutmeg and salt and pepper to taste.

Cover the base of a large tray with a thick layer of semolina. Lay a sheet of pasta on a clean, dry workbench lightly dusted with semolina. If necessary, trim the sides with a pasta wheel to give an 8 cm wide strip. Using the pasta wheel, cut the dough into 8 cm squares. Place a teaspoon of filling in the centre of each square. Using a spray bottle, mist the pasta very lightly with water. Fold each square in half to form a triangle, pressing around the filling to remove as much air as possible. Follow the instructions on page 97 for shaping tortelli. Place in a single layer on the tray and set aside in a cool place until needed.

Bring a large heavy-based saucepan of salted water to the boil. Add the tortelli and cook for 4 minutes or until they rise to the surface and are tender around the edges.

Meanwhile, melt the butter in a small heavy-based frying pan over low heat. As the tortelli rise to the surface, scoop them up with a slotted spoon, drain well, place on a serving platter or divide among plates and sprinkle with the remaining Grana.

Increase the heat under the pan of butter to medium–high and cook until it turns dark nut-brown. Add the sage, toss for 30 seconds or until crisp, then pour over the pasta and serve.

DALLO SPIEDO

FROM THE SPIT

As spit-roasted meat is the most typical Lombardian dish, especially for large gatherings, I was excited to discover I can replicate it in Australia by using the rotisserie attachment of an Aussie barbecue! Cook these recipes over an open grill if possible, but if your barbecue has a flat-plate, remove the trays from that section for the last half hour so the meat or fish cooks evenly. And don't ever leave the spit unattended – pour a drink, get a few friends around for company, then sit back and enjoy!

SPIEDO ALLA BRESCIANA

BRESCIAN-STYLE SPIT-ROASTED MEAT

This is the classic *spiedo* dish from my home province. Ask your butcher to slice the American-cut ribs into segments, butterfly the quail, bone the maryland and slice the pork neck for you – the rest is easy! Here I've divided the meat among five spits (see opposite). The amount of butter is correct as it is used for basting – most of it is discarded.

Serves 10

50 g fine salt

2 sprigs rosemary, leaves very finely chopped

30 thin slices flat pancetta

1 × 1 kg piece pork neck, cut into 10 × 100 g slices

90 large sage leaves

5 quails, butterflied and halved lengthways, rinsed well and patted dry

5 duck marylands, boned and halved lengthways

1 potato, scrubbed and cut in half (optional)

1.2 kg American-cut pork ribs, cut into 7 cm-wide strips, then into segments of 2 bones

1 cup (250 ml) red wine

500 g unsalted butter, melted

Combine the salt and rosemary in a small bowl. Lay 10 slices of pancetta on a clean, dry workbench about 7 cm apart. Lay a slice of pork neck lengthways on each slice of pancetta. Sprinkle with the rosemary salt and top with a sage leaf. Roll the meat up around the sage, then roll the pancetta around the meat. Cover and refrigerate.

Lay another 10 slices of the pancetta on the workbench about 7 cm apart. Lay a quail half on each slice of pancetta. Sprinkle with the rosemary salt and top with a sage leaf. Roll the quail up around the sage, then roll the pancetta around the quail. Cover and refrigerate.

Lay the remaining pancetta slices on the workbench about 7 cm apart. Lay a piece of duck on each slice of pancetta. Sprinkle with rosemary salt and top with a sage leaf. Roll the duck up around the sage, then roll the pancetta around the duck. Cover and refrigerate.

Thread a rotisserie fork (or half a potato), onto the barbecue spit, then a piece of pork neck, a sage leaf, a piece of quail, a sage leaf, a piece of duck, a sage leaf, a piece of pork rib and a sage leaf. Repeat with the remaining meat and sage leaves, finishing with a rotisserie fork or remaining half of the potato), to hold everything firmly in place.

Place over a cold barbecue, place metal trays (disposable foil ones are fine) underneath the spit, then turn the heat on to low. Cook, covered, for 1 hour. Slowly drizzle the wine over the meat, carefully collect it from the trays and drizzle it over the meat again, then discard it from the trays. Sprinkle the meat with half the remaining rosemary salt, increase the heat to medium and cook for another 45 minutes.

Combine the butter and remaining sage leaves in a small heavy-based saucepan over medium heat and cook until the butter has melted. Slowly drizzle half of this over the meat, carefully collect it from the trays and drizzle it over the meat again. Increase the barbecue heat to medium–high and cook for another 30 minutes.

Discard the liquid from the trays, drizzle the meat with the remaining sage butter and collect it from the trays. Sprinkle the meat with the remaining rosemary salt and cook for another 30 minutes. Drizzle the collected butter over the meat, then remove the trays, increase the barbecue heat to high and cook for another 15 minutes.

Remove the meat and serve on a platter. Discard (or eat!) the potato.

QUAGLIE ALLO SPIEDO

QUAILS ROASTED ON A SPIT

In Lombardy we make this with various small birds, including thrush, but here it works very well with quail. If you don't have a rotisserie attachment for your barbecue you can use long metal skewers with two quails per skewer threaded in the same way. Traditionally it's served with polenta – of course – but you could offer salad, boiled potatoes, rice or whatever accompaniment you like alongside. This dish will only be as good as the vinegar you use – you want an authentic Balsamic di Modena, not a cheap imitation. Depending on the width of the pancetta slices you buy, you may not need to use them all.

Serves 8

8 large quails, rinsed well
   and patted dry, brought to
   room temperature
40 thin slices flat pancetta
fine salt
⅓ cup (80 ml) aged Balsamic
   di Modena vinegar, plus extra
   for drizzling
1 radicchio, leaves torn
1 small red onion, thinly sliced
extra virgin olive oil, for drizzling
freshly ground black pepper

Cotechino stuffing

300 g cotechino (see page 225)
50 g fine fresh breadcrumbs
   (see page 226)
50 g unsalted butter, melted

To make the stuffing, wrap the cotechino in foil and pierce with 10 toothpicks evenly spaced over the cotechino. Place in a heavy-based saucepan, cover with cold water and bring to the boil. Reduce the heat to low and simmer, covered, for 3 hours, topping up with boiling water if necessary to keep the cotechino covered. Drain the cotechino, peel it and crumble the meat into a bowl, then add the breadcrumbs and butter and mix well. Set aside.

Divide the stuffing among the quail cavities. Wrap 5 slices of pancetta around each quail, crossing them over on the breast, then truss (see page 227) the quails with kitchen twine.

Arrange the quails in a rotisserie basket, thread the basket onto the barbecue spit and secure firmly. Place over a cold barbecue, place a metal tray underneath the spit (a disposable foil one is fine), then turn the heat on to low. Sprinkle well with salt, then cover and cook for 1 hour 45 minutes, basting every 15 minutes with vinegar and checking that the quails are browning evenly; if not, carefully reposition the basket on the spit. Sprinkle with salt again and cook for another 15 minutes without basting.

Just before serving, combine the radicchio and onion in a bowl and toss with a drizzle of vinegar, a little oil and salt and pepper to taste.

Remove the quails from the spit, cut in half lengthways and serve with the radicchio salad.

GALLETTI ALLO SPIEDO

BABY CHICKENS COOKED ON A SPIT

Spatchcocking is a method of preparing poultry (also called butterflying). You can 'spatchcock' any poultry, but it's a technique so often used on small chickens (what the French call *poussin* and the Italians call *galletti*) that these birds have come to be called spatchcocks. *Pestatina* is our name for the olive oil, garlic and parsley dressing used to baste the birds during cooking, and serve with them afterwards. Use a good cabernet sauvignon or shiraz vinegar for this recipe, not one that's too sharply acidic.

Serves 4

100 ml extra virgin olive oil, plus extra for drizzling

1 handful (about ½ cup) flat-leaf parsley leaves, finely chopped

2 cloves garlic, finely chopped

4 × 500 g spatchcocks, rinsed well and patted dry, brought to room temperature

1 potato, scrubbed and cut in half (optional)

fine salt

100 g wild rocket

6 small red radishes, thinly sliced

cabernet sauvignon vinegar (see page 226), for drizzling
freshly ground black pepper

Herb stuffing

200 g fine fresh breadcrumbs (see page 226)

1 handful (about ½ cup) flat-leaf parsley leaves, chopped

1 tablespoon thyme leaves

4 sprigs rosemary, leaves finely chopped

1 small handful (about ¼ cup) sage leaves, chopped

1 teaspoon fine salt

200 g unsalted butter, cubed

To make the herb stuffing, place the breadcrumbs, parsley, thyme, rosemary, sage and salt in a bowl. Melt the butter in a small heavy-based saucepan over high heat until foaming, then pour over the breadcrumb mixture and mix well.

Combine the oil, parsley and garlic in a bowl, then divide this mixture evenly between two bowls.

Divide the stuffing among the spatchcock cavities.

Thread a rotisserie fork (or half a potato) onto the barbecue spit, then thread the spatchcocks onto the spit, finishing with a rotisserie fork (or remaining half of the potato), to hold everything firmly in place.

Place over a cold barbecue, place a metal tray underneath the spit (a disposable foil one is fine), then turn the heat on to low. Sprinkle the spatchcocks well with salt, then cover and cook for 2 hours 15 minutes, basting every 15 minutes with one bowl of the oil, parsley and garlic mixture and checking that the spatchcocks are securely attached to the spit and browning evenly; if not, carefully reposition them on the spit. Sprinkle with salt again and cook for another 15 minutes without basting.

Just before serving, combine the rocket and radish in a bowl and toss with a drizzle of vinegar, a little oil and salt and pepper to taste.

Remove the spatchcocks from the spit, cut in half lengthways and serve with the rocket salad and remaining bowl of oil, parsley and garlic mixture on the side. Discard (or eat!) the potato.

Pictured clockwise from left: Quails roasted on a spit (page 110);
Roasted baby potatoes (page 140); Baby chickens cooked on a spit
(page 111); Stuffed pigeon cooked on a spit and olive stuffing (page 114)

PICCIONE FARCITO

STUFFED PIGEON COOKED ON A SPIT

When I was small, I didn't like the pigeons that flock around every piazza in Italy looking for something to eat – they were aggressive enough to scare a little boy. It was a long time before I understood that they were the same creatures that my mother cooked, and that are popular all over Italy – in fact, just about all over the world.

Serves 4

4 × 500 g squabs, cleaned, brought to room temperature

28 slices lardo (see page 225)

1 potato, scrubbed and cut in half (optional)

fine salt

150 g unsalted butter, melted

200 ml red wine

Roasted Baby Potatoes (see page 140), to serve

Olive stuffing

250 g sourdough bread, crusts removed, cut into 2 cm dice

100 g pitted Ligurian olives, chopped

salt flakes

100 g unsalted butter

6 sage leaves, finely chopped

To make the olive stuffing, place the bread and olives in a bowl and season with salt to taste. Melt the butter in a heavy-based frying pan over high heat. Add the sage and cook for 3 minutes, then pour over the bread and olives and mix well.

Cut the feet and wing tips off the squabs, remove any fat from the cavity openings and rinse out well with cold water to remove any remaining offal or blood, then pat dry.

Divide the stuffing among the squab cavities. Wrap 7 slices of lardo around the breast of each squab, tuck the heads down onto the breast and truss (see page 227) to secure with kitchen twine.

Thread a rotisserie fork (or half a potato), onto the barbecue spit, thread the squab onto the spit, finishing with a rotisserie fork (or remaining half of the potato), to hold everything firmly in place.

Place over a cold barbecue, place a metal tray underneath the spit (a disposable foil one is fine), then turn the heat on to low. Sprinkle the squabs well with salt, then cover and cook for 2 hours 15 minutes, basting alternately with the melted butter and red wine every 15 minutes and checking that the squabs are securely attached to the spit and browning evenly; if not, carefully reposition them on the spit. Sprinkle with salt again and cook for another 15 minutes without basting.

Remove from the spit, cut each squab in half lengthways and serve with the roasted baby potatoes. Discard (or eat!) the potato.

ANATRA CON LENTICCHIE

SPIT-ROASTED DUCK WITH LENTILS

The cooking method for the lentils may seem a little unusual, as the vegetable *battuta* (see page 16) is deglazed with marsala, before adding the stock, and this mixture is cooked in the oven for 30 minutes to create a delicious braising liquid before adding the lentils. You'll need to start this recipe a day ahead to give the lentils time to soak. There are often a few feathers or quills left in poultry when you buy it. It's best to remove as many of these as possible (see page 226).

Serves 8

1 × 1.7 kg duck, well rinsed and patted dry, brought to room temperature

1 large handful sage (about 1 cup), leaves picked

1 potato, scrubbed and cut in half (optional)

fine salt

2½ cups (500 g) green lentils, soaked in cold water overnight

130 g unsalted butter, cubed

1 white onion, finely chopped

1 carrot, finely chopped

1 stalk celery, finely chopped

1 clove garlic, finely chopped

150 ml marsala

7 sage leaves

5 basil leaves

100 ml Chicken Stock (see page 222)

Cut off and discard the first two joints of the wings (wing tips and wings) and the neck and surrounding skin. Place the sage leaves inside the cavity of the duck and truss with kitchen twine.

Thread a rotisserie fork (or half a potato), onto the barbecue spit, then push the spit through the duck lengthways and finish with a rotisserie fork (or remaining half of the potato), to hold it firmly in place.

Place over a cold barbecue, place a metal tray underneath the spit (a disposable foil one is fine), then turn the heat on to medium. Cover and cook for 30 minutes, then sprinkle liberally with salt. Cook for another 1½ hours, checking occasionally that the duck is securely attached to the spit and browning evenly; if not, carefully reposition it on the spit. Carefully drain the fat from the tray occasionally. Turn the heat off and leave, with the lid closed, for 30 minutes; the duck will continue to cook in the residual heat in this time.

While the duck is cooking, drain the lentils and place in a heavy-based saucepan of cold salted water. Bring to the boil, then reduce the heat to low and simmer for 15–20 minutes or until the lentils are just tender. Drain and set aside.

Preheat the oven to 180°C.

Meanwhile, melt 100 g of the butter in an ovenproof saucepan or flameproof casserole dish over high heat. Add the onion, carrot, celery and garlic, then reduce the heat to medium and cook for 13 minutes or until well browned. Add the marsala, sage, basil and salt to taste, then increase the heat to high and cook for 2–3 minutes or until the marsala has evaporated. Add the stock, return to the boil, then cover and transfer to the oven to bake for 30 minutes. Remove the pan from the oven, add the lentils, then cover and return to the oven for another 45 minutes. Remove from the oven, stir in the remaining butter and set aside in a warm place while you cut the duck.

Cut the duck into 8 pieces, arrange the braised lentils on a platter or on plates, top with the duck and serve. Discard (or eat!) the potato.

ESCE ALLO SPIEDO

WOOD-WRAPPED SPIT-ROASTED FISH

This is not a traditional Lombardian dish, it's one I created when I saw how similar the spit over an Aussie barbecue is to a traditional *spiedo*. In Lombardy, we don't cook fish on the *spiedo*, but I thought why not – Aussies are happy to barbecue anything! Cedar wraps, available from barbecue stores, add a lovely scent and smoky aroma to the fish.

Serves 4

1 × 1.5 kg snapper, gilled, gutted and scaled, tails and fins removed

fine salt

1 lemon, sliced

8 cedar wraps, soaked in cold water for a few minutes

4 sprigs bay leaves

extra virgin olive oil, for drizzling

Wipe out the belly cavity of the snapper with a clean, damp cloth to remove any remaining blood. Salt the fish generously inside and out and place the lemon slices in the belly cavity.

Line a rotisserie basket with cedar wraps, place 2 sprigs of bay leaves on top, then the snapper, remaining bay leaves and more cedar wraps. Close the cage as tightly as possible to secure the fish.

Thread the basket onto the barbecue spit and secure firmly. Place over a cold barbecue, place a metal tray underneath the spit (a disposable foil one is fine), then turn the heat on to low. Cover and cook for 40 minutes, checking often to ensure the basket is turning smoothly; if not, carefully reposition it on the spit. Remove the basket from the spit and set aside in a warm place for the fish to rest for 10 minutes.

Remove the snapper from the basket, then place the whole fish on a platter, or shred the flesh into a bowl, drizzle with oil and serve.

PORCHETTA ALLO SPIEDO

PORK BELLY ROASTED ON THE SPIT WITH APPLE SALAD

This is the perfect dish to serve a crowd, and makes a great centrepiece for a gathering of family and friends. I like to dry-age all meat, in particular pork belly, because it helps to make the skin crisp. Order the pork belly one week in advance and ask your butcher to dry-age it for you. This dish can be eaten hot or cold, and is delicious thinly sliced in a *panino* (bread roll).

Serves 12

1 × 2 kg pork belly, skin on

500 g fine salt

2 tablespoons salt flakes

½ teaspoon freshly ground black pepper

10 sprigs rosemary, leaves finely chopped

1 potato, scrubbed and cut in half (optional)

Apple salad

2 red apples

4 large handfuls (about 4 cups) lamb's ear lettuce

100 g Grana Padano, freshly shaved

chardonnay vinegar (see page 226), for drizzling

extra virgin olive oil, for drizzling

salt flakes and freshly ground black pepper

Place the pork on a tray, skin-side up, and cover the skin with fine salt. Refrigerate for 6 hours, then brush off the salt.

To butterfly the pork, slice it widthways almost all the way through. Open it up and spread the salt flakes, pepper and rosemary over the flesh. Roll it up like a Swiss roll, as tightly as possible so that only the skin is showing on the outside, if possible. Loop a piece of kitchen twine lengthways around the centre of the roll and tie it, then turn the roll 90° and loop the twine around again. Tie it off, then tie around the circumference of the roll at 4 cm intervals. When you get to the end, go back the other way, placing the twine diagonally between each section.

Thread a rotisserie fork (or half a potato), onto the barbecue spit, then thread the rolled pork on lengthways and finish with a rotisserie fork (or remaining half of the potato), to hold it firmly in place.

Place over a cold barbecue, place a metal tray underneath the spit (a disposable aluminium one is fine), then turn the heat on to low. Cover and cook for 1 hour 45 minutes, checking occasionally that the roll is securely attached to the spit and browning evenly; if not, carefully reposition the pork on the spit. Increase the heat to medium, poke holes in the skin with a carving fork to release some of the fat (this will help crisp the skin), and cook for another 2 hours. Turn the heat off and leave, with the lid closed, for 30 minutes; the pork will continue to cook in the residual heat in this time.

Meanwhile, to make the apple salad, thinly slice the apples and combine with the lettuce, Grana, a drizzle each of vinegar and oil, and salt and pepper to taste.

Remove the twine from the pork, cut into 1 cm-thick slices and serve with the apple salad. Discard (or eat!) the potato.

SPALLA DI AGNELLO SALLO SPIEDO

LAMB SHOULDER COOKED ON THE SPIT

Be warned, once you've tried this, you'll never look at the Sunday roast lamb the same way again! You'll need to start this recipe two days before you cook it to give the lamb time to marinate. Ask your butcher to cut the end of the leg bone off the shoulder so that the spit will be able to turn freely above the barbecue plate.

Serves 4

1 × 2 kg lamb shoulder, leg bone cut off

2 tablespoons fine salt, plus extra for sprinkling

1 potato, scrubbed and cut in half (optional)

250 g baby green beans, topped and tailed

extra virgin olive oil, for drizzling

1 clove garlic, thinly sliced

1 large handful (about 1 cup) flat-leaf parsley leaves, chopped

1 small handful (about ¼ cup) mint leaves, finely chopped

Marinade

2 litres red wine

4 star anise

2 sticks cinnamon

1 carrot, roughly chopped

1 onion, roughly chopped

1 stalk celery, roughly chopped

1 sprig rosemary, leaves finely chopped

5 black peppercorns, lightly crushed

To make the marinade, combine the wine, star anise, cinnamon, carrot, onion, celery, rosemary and peppercorns in a bowl large enough to also fit the lamb. Place the lamb in the marinade, then cover and refrigerate for 48 hours, turning occasionally if it isn't fully submerged.

Remove the lamb from the marinade, pat dry and set aside for 30 minutes to bring to room temperature. Reserve the marinade for basting.

Rub the salt into the lamb. Loop a piece of kitchen twine lengthways around the centre of the meat and tie it, then turn it 90° and loop the twine around again to form a long roll shape. Tie it off, then tie around the outside of the roll at 4 cm intervals. When you get to the end, go back the other way, placing the twine diagonally between each section.

Thread a rotisserie fork, or half a potato onto the barbecue spit, then thread the roll on lengthways and finish with a rotisserie fork (or remaining half of the potato), to hold it firmly in place.

Place over a cold barbecue, place a metal tray underneath the spit (a disposable foil one is fine), then turn the heat on to low. Cover and cook for 1 hour 45 minutes, basting with the marinade every 15 minutes and checking that the roll is securely attached to the spit and browning evenly; if not, carefully reposition the lamb on the spit. Increase the barbecue heat to medium and cook for another 45 minutes, basting every 15 minutes. Sprinkle with salt and cook for another 15 minutes without basting. Turn the heat off and leave, with the lid closed, for 30 minutes; the lamb will continue to cook in the residual heat in this time.

Meanwhile, blanch the beans in a saucepan of boiling salted water for 8 minutes or until tender. Drain well and toss with a drizzle of oil and the garlic, parsley and mint.

Remove the twine from the lamb, place on a platter and serve the beans in a bowl. To serve, shred the meat from the lamb shoulder using a spoon and fork and place on diners' plates. Discard (or eat!) the potato.

122

COSTOLETTE DI MANZO ALLO SPIEDO

BEEF SHORT RIBS COOKED ON A SPIT

Short ribs are wide, flat bones that sit at the base of a piece of tender, fatty meat – not exactly low in kilojoules, but very tasty. Once this is cooked, you slice the meat off the bones, though my brother and I always loved gnawing on the bones as much as we enjoyed the meat itself. You'll need to start this recipe at least three hours before you want to cook it in order to marinate the meat, but it's best to marinate it in the refrigerator overnight if you have time.

Serves 6

2 kg beef short ribs

1 small handful (about ¼ cup) thyme leaves, finely chopped

1 potato, scrubbed and cut in half (optional)

fine salt

Balsamic marinade

1 litre water

200 ml aged Balsamic di Modena vinegar

1 carrot, diced

1 stalk celery, diced

1 red onion, diced

5 black peppercorns

1 fresh bay leaf

30 g caster sugar

To make the balsamic marinade, place the water, vinegar, carrot, celery, onion, peppercorns, bay leaf and sugar in a heavy-based saucepan, bring to the boil, then remove from the heat. Set aside to cool to room temperature, then refrigerate until cold.

Place the ribs in a glass or ceramic container just large enough to hold them and the marinade, then pour over the marinade. Cover and refrigerate for at least 3 hours, preferably overnight, turning occasionally if they aren't fully submerged.

Remove the beef from the marinade and discard the marinade. Pat the beef dry, then set aside for 30 minutes to bring to room temperature. Rub the thyme into the beef.

Thread a rotisserie fork (or half a potato) onto the barbecue spit, then thread the spit through the ribs lengthways and finish with a rotisserie fork (or remaining half of the potato), to hold it firmly in place.

Place over a cold barbecue, place a metal tray underneath the spit (a disposable foil one is fine), then turn the heat on to medium. Cover and cook for 30 minutes, then sprinkle liberally with salt. Cook for another 1½ hours, occasionally carefully draining the fat from the tray and checking that the meat is securely attached to the spit and browning evenly; if not, carefully reposition the ribs on the spit. Turn the heat off and leave, with the lid closed, for 30 minutes; the ribs will continue to cook in the residual heat in this time.

Cut the meat into thick slices, arrange on a platter and serve.

Clockwise from left: Beef short ribs cooked on a spit (page 123);
Spit-roasted veal shanks (page 126); Lamb shoulder cooked
on the spit (page 122)

STINCO DI VITELLO ALLO SPIEDO

SPIT-ROASTED VEAL SHANKS

We love veal shanks in Lombardy, although traditionally they would be cooked in the oven not on the spit. We do cook pork shanks on the *spiedo*, and I've discovered that veal works just as well. Of course, you could serve soft polenta (see page 49) with this, but some good crusty bread would also work – and leftovers are great the next day cold in a *panino* (bread roll).

Serves 6

2 × 750 g veal shanks, brought to room temperature

3 sprigs rosemary, leaves very finely chopped

1 potato, scrubbed and cut in half (optional)

fine salt

Rub the shanks all over with the rosemary.

Thread a rotisserie fork (or half a potato) onto the barbecue spit, then push the spit through the meat of the shanks lengthways and finish with a rotisserie fork (or remaining half of the potato), to hold them firmly in place.

Place over a cold barbecue, place a metal tray underneath the spit (a disposable foil one is fine), then turn the heat on to medium. Cover and cook for 30 minutes, then sprinkle liberally with salt. Cook for another 1½ hours, occasionally carefully draining the fat from the tray and checking that the shanks are securely attached to the spit and browning evenly; if not, carefully reposition the shanks on the spit. Turn the heat off and leave, with the lid closed, for 30 minutes; the shanks will continue to cook in the residual heat in this time.

Shred the meat from the shanks, arrange on a platter and serve.

DAL FORNO

FROM THE OVEN

In Lombardy, as recently as the early 1900s, cooking was mostly done over an open fireplace. The only ovens were communal wood-fired ones in the *piazza* or the bakery. Today home-baking is popular, especially for large cuts of meat and braises. A few important tips for tender juicy results: bring food to room temperature before cooking it, check towards the end of the cooking time (as every oven is different), and rest meat for 10–15 minutes after cooking.

TINCA RIPIENA ALL'ISEANA

STUFFED BAKED BARRAMUNDI

This dish is traditionally cooked in a terracotta pot, using *tinca* (tench), a freshwater fish from the Lombardian lakes that was introduced to Australia and is now found in freshwater lakes and rivers in south-eastern Australia. It lives among the weeds and can have a slightly muddy flavour – traditionally cooks would spoon vinegar into the mouths of live fish to help counteract this. Tench can be hard to buy in Australia, so I've used barramundi here, and Murray cod is also good cooked this way. If you have a bay tree, use small twigs of bay leaves as a base for the fish. This recipe uses a lot of butter – that's the way we like it in Lombardy!

Serves 4

4 × 500 g barramundi, gilled, gutted and scaled

extra virgin olive oil, for drizzling

fine fresh breadcrumbs (see page 226), for dusting

4 sprigs fresh bay leaves

400 g unsalted butter, cubed

Grilled Polenta (see page 54), to serve

Stuffing

150 g unsalted butter

1 clove garlic, finely chopped

1 small handful (about ¼ cup) flat-leaf parsley, leaves picked

fine salt

150 g fine fresh breadcrumbs (see page 226)

100 g Grana Padano, freshly grated

2½ tablespoons Chicken Stock (see page 222), as needed

freshly ground black pepper

To make the stuffing, melt the butter in a small heavy-based frying pan over high heat and cook until golden brown. Add the garlic, parsley and salt to taste, then fry for 1–2 minutes or until the garlic is lightly coloured.

Combine the breadcrumbs and Grana in a bowl. Mix the garlic mixture into the breadcrumb mixture, then stir in just enough stock to bring the mixture together; you may not need it all. Season with salt and pepper to taste.

Preheat the oven to 220°C.

Remove the tails and fins from the fish. Wipe out the belly cavities of the fish with a clean, damp cloth to remove any remaining blood. Pack one-quarter of the stuffing into each of the belly cavities. Tie the fish securely with three loops of kitchen twine to keep the stuffing in place. Drizzle with the oil and dust with breadcrumbs.

Place 2 of the bay sprigs evenly in a single layer in a baking dish and place the fish on top, belly-side down. Dot evenly with the butter and top with the remaining bay sprigs. Cover tightly with foil and bake for 30 minutes, basting occasionally with the pan juices.

Uncover and bake for another 10–15 minutes or until the fish are cooked through. Remove from the oven, cover and set aside to rest for 10 minutes.

Divide the fish among plates and serve with the grilled polenta.

ROTA RIPIENA CON FUNGHI

RAINBOW TROUT FILLED WITH MUSHROOMS

You can use any mushrooms for this dish – I love it in Italy with slippery jacks when they're in season, but I've also used the large flat cultivated mushrooms widely available here in Australia.

Serves 6

200 g unsalted butter

200 ml extra virgin olive oil, plus extra for drizzling

1 white onion, finely chopped

3 cloves garlic, 2 finely chopped, 1 bruised

350 g flat mushrooms, stalks discarded, diced

1 handful (about ½ cup) flat-leaf parsley leaves, chopped

½ cup (125 ml) Chicken Stock (see page 222)

1 cup (140 g) fine fresh breadcrumbs (see page 226)

50 g Grana Padano, freshly grated

salt flakes and freshly ground black pepper

6 × 180 g rainbow trout fillets, skin on, pin-boned

18 thin slices prosciutto (see page 226)

Melt 100 g of the butter in a heavy-based frying pan over high heat. Add 100 ml of the oil and, when hot, add the onion and chopped garlic, then cook for 1–2 minutes or until it starts to colour. Add the mushroom and cook for 2 minutes or until it starts to soften. Stir in the parsley, remove from the heat and set aside.

Place the remaining butter and bruised garlic in a heavy-based frying pan and cook for a minute or 2 until the butter is light brown. Add the stock and bring to the boil, then remove from the heat.

Stir the breadcrumbs and Grana into the mushroom mixture, season to taste with salt and pepper and add enough of the stock mixture to just bring it all together, mixing with your hands and discarding the bruised garlic.

Check the fish for any remaining scales and remove. Sprinkle the flesh side well with salt and pepper. Place three 40 cm strips of plastic film lengthways on a clean, dry workbench. Arrange 6 of the prosciutto slices widthways in a slightly overlapping row on each sheet of plastic film to create a bed for the fish. Place a fish fillet, skin-side down, in the centre of each prosciutto 'bed', then pack one-third of the filling onto each one. Top with a second fillet, skin-side up, facing in the opposite direction. Use the plastic film to lift the prosciutto over the fish, then roll tightly in the plastic film and refrigerate for at least 30 minutes. (The fish can be prepared to this stage and refrigerated for up to 24 hours in advance of cooking. Just remove it from the refrigerator to come to room temperature 30 minutes before cooking.)

Preheat the oven to 220°C.

Unwrap the fish parcels, discarding the plastic film. Heat the remaining oil in a heavy-based non-stick frying pan over high heat. Add the fish parcels and cook for 30 seconds on each side or until well coloured. Transfer the fish parcels to a baking tray (or use an ovenproof frying pan) and bake for 6 minutes; the fish should be cooked through.

Remove from the oven, cover the fish loosely with foil and set aside in a warm place for 5 minutes. Slice the fish parcels into portions, arrange on a platter, drizzle with extra oil and serve.

PESCE IN CROSTA DI PROSCIUTTO E CAVOLO

PROSCIUTTO-CRUSTED MURRAY COD WITH CABBAGE TWO WAYS

Cabbage with prosciutto is a classic combo, but here I take it up a notch or two. You'll need to buy a whole Savoy cabbage to get enough outer leaves for this recipe, but you'll only use a quarter of the centre, so the rest can be made into coleslaw.

Place the prosciutto in a heavy-based non-stick frying pan over medium heat and cook for 15 minutes or until crisp. Drain on paper towel.

To make the braised cabbage, heat the oil and butter in a large heavy-based saucepan over medium heat. Add the onion and cook for 5–10 minutes or until soft. Add the cabbage and reduce the heat to low. Cook, covered, stirring occasionally, for 35 minutes or until the cabbage is soft but not coloured; if it starts to stick add a couple of tablespoons of water, then finish cooking uncovered. Cover and set aside to keep warm. Warm gently just before serving, if necessary.

To make the cabbage purée, bring a large heavy-based saucepan of salted water to the boil. Add the cabbage and cook for 15 minutes or until the hard white stalk is tender. Transfer to a blender with salt and pepper to taste. Reserve the cooking water to use if needed. With the motor running, slowly drizzle in the olive oil and, if necessary, enough of the cooking water to create a smooth, creamy purée. Taste and add salt and pepper, if needed. Place in a bowl over a bowl of iced water and stir to cool as quickly as possible to retain the vibrant colour.

Preheat the oven to 180°C.

Sprinkle the fish with salt and pepper on both sides and drizzle with extra oil. Heat the oil in a heavy-based frying pan over medium heat and, when hot, add the fish, skin-side down, then cook for 2 minutes or until lightly golden. Transfer the fish, skin-side down, to a baking tray lined with baking paper (or use an ovenproof frying pan).

Bake the fish for 6 minutes or until it is almost cooked through; it should still be rare in the centre (46°C on a probe thermometer; see page 227). Remove the fish from the oven, leaving the oven on. Drizzle the fish with extra oil and gently press the prosciutto on top, then return to the oven for 4 minutes or until the fish is just cooked through (50°C on the thermometer).

Gently warm the cabbage purée in a heavy-based saucepan over low heat. Spread a spoonful of cabbage purée on each plate, top with a spoonful of braised cabbage and a piece of fish, then drizzle with extra oil and serve.

Serves 6

350 g prosciutto (see page 226), cut into 2 mm-thick slices (ask your deli to do this), fat discarded, cut into 3 mm dice

6 × 200 g pieces Murray cod fillet, skin off, pin-boned, removed from the refrigerator 30 minutes before cooking to come to room temperature

salt flakes and freshly ground white pepper

50 ml extra virgin olive oil, plus extra for drizzling

Braised cabbage

¼ cup (60 ml) extra virgin olive oil

50 g unsalted butter

1 large onion, very thinly sliced

¼ Savoy cabbage, white centre only, finely shredded

Cabbage purée

rock salt

1 Savoy cabbage, outer green leaves only

salt flakes and freshly ground white pepper

1½ tablespoons extra virgin olive oil

135

TAROZ
POTATO, CHEESE AND BEAN PIE

Serves 2–4

fine salt

2 floury potatoes, such as russet (about 400 g), peeled and diced

200 g green beans, topped and tailed

75 g unsalted butter, plus extra for buttering

1 small white onion, thinly sliced

1 pinch of freshly grated nutmeg

fine salt and freshly ground black pepper

200 g fontina, sliced

green salad, to serve

This pie is usually served in the middle of the table as a light meal to share, or it could be a side dish for four people alongside grilled meats.

Preheat the oven to 180°C.

Bring a large heavy-based saucepan of salted water to the boil. Add the potato and beans, reduce the heat to medium and simmer for 20 minutes or until tender.

Meanwhile, melt the butter in a heavy-based frying pan over medium heat. Add the onion and cook for 10 minutes or until golden.

Drain the potato and beans, place in a heatproof bowl and season with nutmeg and salt and pepper to taste. Mash together to form a coarse paste. Stir in the onion mixture, then spread half into a buttered baking dish. Top with 100 g of the fontina, then add the remaining mixture and top with the remaining fontina. Bake for 10 minutes or until the cheese has melted and become golden brown.

Serve hot with a green salad on the side.

MELANZANE ALLA COMASCO
BEEF AND BÉCHAMEL STUFFED EGGPLANT

Serves 8

50 g unsalted butter, plus extra for buttering

½ onion, finely chopped

300 g beef mince

75 ml dry white wine

1 egg, lightly beaten

100 g Grana Padano, freshly grated

200 g fine fresh breadcrumbs (see page 226)

4 eggplants (aubergines), halved lengthways, seeds scooped out and discarded

fine salt

3 bulbs baby fennel, shaved

This dish, from the Como province, is the Lombardian equivalent of eggplant Parmigiana; of course in Lombardy, we add meat! Or, with the creamy béchamel, it's a bit like a lasagne without the pasta.

To make the béchamel sauce, bring the milk to the boil in a small heavy-based saucepan. Meanwhile, melt the butter in a small heavy-based saucepan over medium heat, then add the flour and cook for 5 minutes, whisking constantly. Whisk in the milk, in three or four batches, and continue whisking until it comes to a simmer. Reduce the heat to low and whisk for another 2 minutes. Stir in the salt and nutmeg and set aside.

Melt the butter in a heavy-based frying pan over medium heat. Add the onion and cook for 5 minutes or until soft. Add the mince and increase the heat to high, then cook for 5 minutes or until well coloured. Add the wine, stir to combine well and cook for 1 minute or until the wine has evaporated, then stir in the béchamel sauce. Remove from the heat and set aside for 10 minutes to cool a little. Stir in the egg, Grana and 100 g of the breadcrumbs and refrigerate for 30 minutes or until firm. »

extra virgin olive oil, for drizzling

½ lemon

freshly ground black pepper

Béchamel sauce

400 ml milk

35 g unsalted butter

¼ cup (35 g) plain flour

fine salt

1 pinch of freshly grated nutmeg

Preheat the oven to 200°C.

Sprinkle the eggplant flesh with salt, turn upside down on a wire rack over a tray to catch the juices and set aside for 10 minutes to drain. Rinse the eggplant under cold water and pat dry. Cut a thin slice off the base of the skin side of each half so it sits flat, then place in a buttered baking dish that fits them snugly in one layer. Spoon the meat mixture into the hollow of the eggplant halves and sprinkle with the remaining breadcrumbs. Bake for 30–40 minutes or until the topping is well browned and they are tender.

Meanwhile, toss the fennel with a drizzle of olive oil and a squeeze of lemon juice, then season with salt and pepper to taste. Serve half an eggplant per person with the fennel salad on the side.

CAPÙ DELLA NONNA MARIA
STUFFED CABBAGE LEAVES

Serves 4

6 large Savoy cabbage leaves

salt flakes

2 cloves garlic, peeled

1 handful (about ½ cup) flat-leaf parsley leaves

40 g unsalted butter

½ onion, finely diced

50 g flat pancetta, finely diced

250 g beef mince

150 g Grana Padano, freshly grated

100 g fine fresh breadcrumbs (see page 226)

2 eggs, lightly beaten

1 pinch of freshly grated nutmeg

¼ cup (60 ml) extra virgin olive oil, plus extra for drizzling

300 g tinned whole, peeled Italian tomatoes, chopped

freshly ground black pepper

Mamma sometimes makes this recipe, inherited from her mother, into six larger rolls using whole leaves, in which case you only need one or two rolls per person. This is great for using the outside leaves of a cabbage when the tender inside leaves have been eaten in a salad. It's also good to make ahead and reheat as it stays moist and delicious.

Blanch the cabbage leaves, in two batches, in a saucepan of boiling salted water for 5 minutes. Pat dry and lay out on a clean, dry workbench, then cut in half along the central rib. Finely chop the garlic and parsley together.

Melt the butter in a heavy-based frying pan over medium heat, then add the garlic and parsley mixture and half of the onion and cook for 2 minutes. Add the pancetta and cook for another 2 minutes. Add the mince and cook for 4 minutes, then transfer to a bowl and set aside to cool for a few minutes. Add the Grana, breadcrumbs, egg and nutmeg and mix with your hands until well combined.

Divide the mixture among the cabbage leaves. Fold each leaf around the meat mixture, tucking in the ends to enclose, then tie with kitchen twine or cotton (like a ribbon around a parcel) and set aside.

Preheat the oven to 180°C.

Heat a large ovenproof frying pan over medium heat. Add the oil and, when hot, add the remaining onion and cook for 1–2 minutes or until soft. Add the tomato and any juices and bring to the boil, then reduce the heat to low and season with salt and pepper. Add the cabbage rolls to the pan in a single layer. Cover tightly with foil and transfer to the oven to bake for 20 minutes.

Remove the rolls from the sauce, snip off the twine and serve with the sauce poured over the top and an extra drizzle of oil.

Pictured from left: Potato, cheese and bean pie (page 136);
Beef and béchamel stuffed eggplant (page 136);
Stuffed cabbage leaves (page 137)

CAPRETTO ALLA BRESCIANA

ROASTED KID WITH ROASTED BABY POTATOES

This is one of my family's favourite recipes, and we also cook rabbit and baby lamb the same way. You'll need to start this the day before cooking to give the goat time to marinate. You may need to order the goat from your butcher in advance. I like to use a shoulder quarter as it has more flavour and more fat than the leg, so it stays moist during the long cooking; the meat literally falls off the bone when it's ready. Vic's Meat sells quarter baby goats, which can be airfreighted: vicsmeat.com.au.

Serves 6

1 large onion, finely chopped

4 cloves garlic, finely chopped

5 sprigs rosemary, leaves finely chopped

1 small handful (about ¼ cup) sage leaves, chopped

100 ml extra virgin olive oil, plus extra for pan-frying

1 baby goat quarter (2.2 kg), cleaned and cut into 18 pieces

1½ tablespoons salt flakes

200 g unsalted butter, diced

freshly ground black pepper

Roasted baby potatoes

800 g baby new potatoes, scrubbed and cut into halves or quarters, depending on size

rock salt, as needed

¼ cup (60 ml) extra virgin olive oil

3 sprigs rosemary, leaves finely chopped

1 clove garlic, finely chopped

Combine the onion, garlic, rosemary, sage and oil in a large bowl. Add the goat, mix well to coat, then cover and refrigerate overnight.

Preheat the oven to 160°C.

Remove the goat from the refrigerator and set aside for 30 minutes to bring to room temperature, then stir the salt through. Place in a large roasting tin or baking dish, dot with the butter and season with pepper to taste, then cover with foil and roast for 2 hours.

Meanwhile, to prepare the roasted baby potatoes, place the potatoes in a large heavy-based saucepan of salted water and bring to the boil. Cook for 5 minutes. Drain and pat dry. Toss with the oil, rosemary and garlic, then transfer to a baking dish and set aside.

Remove the goat from the oven, remove the foil and drain the liquid from the roasting tin or baking dish.

Increase the oven temperature to 220°C, then return the tin or dish to the oven, uncovered, for 30 minutes or until the goat is well coloured. Place the potatoes in the oven to roast at the same time.

Serve the goat on a platter surrounded by the roasted potatoes.

MANZO ALLA CALIFORNIA

BEEF CALIFORNIA-STYLE

Despite the name, this is a very traditional Lombardian dish. California is a small town near Monza, where the Ferrari racing track is – the Ferrari California car is named for this town, not for the American state. Perhaps the more famous American state was named for this town? Larding is a technique that adds moisture and flavour to meat by weaving strips of fat through it using a larding needle. You'll need to buy a larding needle from a kitchenware store. If you can, lard the meat the night before you want to cook it so some of the flavour of the pancetta goes into the meat. Ask your butcher to trim a whole oyster blade of fat and the membrane under the fat, called 'silverskin'; this should leave you with about 1.5 kg of meat.

Serves 8

1 × 50 g piece flat pancetta, cut into 5-mm thick strips

1 × 1.5 kg beef oyster blade, already trimmed of fat and membrane

30 g unsalted butter

1 onion, finely chopped

fine salt

grapeseed oil, for drizzling and pan-frying

plain flour, for dusting

⅓ cup (80 ml) chardonnay vinegar (see page 226)

700 ml milk

1 tablespoon cornflour, dissolved in 1 tablespoon cold water

Borlotti Beans with Pork Skin (see page 24), to serve

crusty bread, to serve

Preheat the oven to 220°C.

Ideally the day before cooking, use a larding needle to thread strips of pancetta through the beef, then cover and refrigerate until 1 hour before you're ready to cook it.

Melt the butter in a heavy-based frying pan, then add the onion and cook over medium heat for 10 minutes or until soft.

Meanwhile, sprinkle the beef liberally with salt, rub with a drizzle of oil and dust with flour. Heat another large heavy-based frying pan over high heat, add a little oil and the meat and cook for 3–4 minutes on each side, until browned all over. Transfer to a baking dish and set aside.

Add the vinegar to the onion and cook over high heat for 1–2 minutes or until evaporated, then add 350 ml of the milk and stir well to remove any bits stuck to the bottom of the pan; the vinegar will cause the milk to curdle, but this is fine. Bring to the boil and pour over the beef.

Cover the beef tightly with foil and roast for 2 hours, basting with the pan juices after 1 hour. Reduce the oven temperature to 120°C and roast for another 30 minutes or until the beef almost starts to fall apart. Remove the beef from the pan and cut into thick slices, then arrange on a platter. Cover and set aside in a warm place.

Transfer the cooking juices to a small heavy-based saucepan and bring to the boil, then add the remaining milk and return to the boil. Add the cornflour mixture and whisk until thickened. Pour some of this sauce over the meat and serve the remainder in a jug for those who would like extra sauce.

Serve with the borlotti beans with pork skin and crusty bread.

142

TRACOTTO

BEEF BRAISED IN RED WINE

My *nonna* used to make this old-fashioned dish with donkey meat – I've adapted it for Australia by using oyster blade steak. The quality of the wine will dictate the quality of this dish – we would use a Barolo or a Barbera in Italy. You could use an Australian shiraz or cabernet sauvignon, not a light wine like chianti or pinot noir. This would traditionally be served with soft polenta (see page 49) – of course! Start this recipe a day ahead of cooking to give the meat time to marinate.

Serves 6

1 litre heavy red wine, plus extra
   if needed to cover

4 onions, chopped

1 carrot, chopped

1 stalk celery, chopped

2 cloves garlic, chopped

1 small leek, white part only,
   washed well, chopped

2 sprigs rosemary

2 sprigs thyme

6 juniper berries

2 cloves

2 fresh bay leaves

10 black peppercorns

1 × 2 cm piece cinnamon stick

2 star anise

1 × 1.5 kg beef oyster blade,
   already trimmed of fat
   and membrane

plain flour, for dusting

100 ml extra virgin olive oil,
   plus extra for drizzling

1 × 200 g piece flat pancetta,
   cut into 2 cm cubes

2 litres Chicken Stock
   (see page 222)

¼ cup (35 g) cornflour

¼ cup (60 ml) cold water

Combine the wine, onion, carrot, celery, garlic, leek, rosemary, thyme, juniper, cloves, bay leaves, peppercorns, cinnamon and star anise in a large glass or ceramic container. Submerge the beef in the marinade; if it's not completely covered, add a little more wine, then weight it down with a plate if necessary. Cover tightly and refrigerate for 24 hours.

Remove the beef from the marinade and strain the marinade, reserving the wine, vegetables and garlic separately and discarding the herbs and spices. Set aside for 30 minutes to bring to room temperature.

Meanwhile, preheat the oven to 230°C.

Pat the beef dry and dust with flour. Heat a flameproof roasting tin over high heat, add a drizzle of extra oil and the beef and cook for 3–4 minutes on each side or until well coloured. Set aside.

Heat a heavy-based saucepan over medium heat, add the oil and, when hot, add the reserved vegetables. Cook for 10–12 minutes or until they start to colour, then add the pancetta and cook for another 4 minutes. Transfer the vegetable mixture to the roasting tin with the beef, then pour over the stock and reserved wine and bring to the boil over high heat. Remove from the heat and cover tightly with foil.

Transfer to the oven to cook for 2 hours, checking occasionally to ensure the beef isn't drying out; turn and baste it occasionally, if necessary. Reduce the oven temperature to 120°C and cook for another 30 minutes.

Transfer the beef to a plate, cover with foil and set aside.

Strain the cooking liquid into a heavy-based frying pan, discarding the solids, then bring to the boil over high heat. Simmer over medium heat for 30 minutes. Stir the cornflour and water in a small bowl until the cornflour dissolves. Gradually add the cornflour mixture to the sauce and whisk until slightly thickened, then cook, stirring occasionally, for another 10 minutes. Slice the meat and return it the sauce, then bring to the boil to warm it through.

Arrange the meat on a platter, cover with the sauce and serve.

MANZO ALL'OLIO DI ROVATO

BEEF WITH ANCHOVY AND OLIVE OIL

This is a very famous recipe from Rovato, a village about 20 minutes from my home town known for its live cattle market, held there on the last Friday of the month for hundreds of years. Farmers and butchers travel from all over Lombardy – the butchers choose their cattle when they are calves and then take delivery of them when they're fully grown. Franciacorta would be the typical wine used in this dish. Although traditionally the meat is not browned, I think it has a better flavour this way. This dish is great served with the crisp rice cake on page 61.

Serves 8

50 g unsalted butter

1 × 1.5 kg piece beef oyster blade, already trimmed of fat and membrane, brought to room temperature

60 g (about 10) anchovy fillets in olive oil, drained

2 cloves garlic, finely chopped

1 small white onion, finely chopped

3 litres water

salt flakes

200 ml extra virgin olive oil, plus extra for drizzling

50 g fine fresh breadcrumbs (see page 226)

⅓ cup (50 g) cornflour, mixed to a paste with a little cold water

freshly ground black pepper

1 handful (about ½ cup) flat-leaf parsley leaves, chopped

30 g Grana Padano, freshly grated

mixed leaf salad, to serve

Preheat the oven to 180°C.

Melt the butter in a deep flameproof roasting tin over medium heat. Add the beef and cook for 3–4 minutes on each side or until well browned. Remove the beef from the tin and set aside.

Add the anchovies, garlic and onion to the tin and cook for 5 minutes or until soft but not coloured. Add the water and a pinch of salt and bring to the boil. Return the beef to the tin and add a little extra water if necessary so that it is just covered. Return to the boil, then reduce the heat to low, cover tightly with foil and transfer to the oven to roast for 2 hours.

Reduce the oven temperature to 120°C and cook for another 30 minutes or until the beef almost starts to fall apart. Remove the beef from the sauce, then cover and set aside in a warm place.

Place the tin over low heat. Slowly pour all the oil into the cooking liquid, whisking constantly, then whisk in the breadcrumbs and cornflour paste. Increase the heat to high and whisk until boiling. Return the beef to the tin, reduce the heat to low and cook for another 30 minutes, stirring often to prevent the beef from sticking.

Remove the beef from the tin, then cover and set aside in a warm place. Increase the heat to low–medium and simmer the sauce for 1 hour or until it is reduced to the consistency of thickened cream. Taste and season with salt and pepper.

Cut the meat into 1 cm-thick slices, return to the sauce and bring to the boil to warm it through.

Arrange the meat on a platter, cover with the sauce and scatter with the parsley and Grana. Drizzle with extra oil and serve with the salad and any remaining sauce on the side for those who like a little extra.

FEGATO ALLA LODIGIANA

VEAL LIVER WRAPPED IN PROSCIUTTO

My brother, Nicola, always refused to eat liver, but when our mother cooked it this way, wrapped in prosciutto and flavoured with fennel seeds, he loved it – though *Mamma* didn't tell him it was liver until after he'd eaten it all! Ask your butcher to slice the liver for you.

Serves 6

1½ teaspoons fennel seeds

18 thin slices prosciutto (see page 226)

18 × 60 g slices veal liver, brought to room temperature

100 g unsalted butter

salt flakes

boiled baby potatoes, to serve

Toast the fennel seeds in a small dry heavy-based frying pan for 2 minutes or until aromatic. Using a pestle, crush lightly in a mortar.

Preheat the oven to 200°C.

Lay the prosciutto slices out on a clean, dry workbench, then place a slice of liver on top of each one. Sprinkle the liver evenly with fennel seeds and roll it up, then roll the prosciutto around it. Secure with a toothpick.

Melt the butter in a large ovenproof frying pan over high heat. Add the liver rolls and cook for 1 minute on each side or until well browned. Transfer to the oven and cook for 5 minutes or until the liver is cooked but still pink in the centre.

Sprinkle with salt to taste and serve with boiled potatoes.

OSSIBUCHI

Ossibuchi (*ossobuco* in the singular), literally meaning 'hollow bones', is a section of a veal shank cut about 3 cm thick. Available from most butchers, this cut has a layer of meat attached and the marrow still in the bones – though often they are so large I'm sure they are from beef, not veal. This is traditionally served with Risotto Milanese (see page 60), which also contains bone marrow.

Serves 6

6 pieces of veal ossobuco, brought to room temperature

plain flour, for dusting

¼ cup (60 ml) grapeseed oil

salt flakes and freshly ground black pepper

60 g unsalted butter

½ small white onion, diced

½ stalk celery, diced

½ small carrot, diced

20 g prosciutto (see page 226), diced

1 cup (250 ml) dry white wine

150 g tinned whole, peeled Italian tomatoes, chopped

1 litre Chicken Stock (see page 222), as needed, to cover

Risotto Milanese (see page 60), to serve

Gremolata

1 handful (about ½ cup) flat-leaf parsley leaves, finely chopped

finely grated zest of ½ lemon

1 clove garlic, crushed

Preheat the oven to 180°C.

Dust the veal with the flour, shaking off the excess.

Heat the oil in a deep ovenproof frying pan over high heat. Working in batches if necessary, add the veal, sprinkle with salt and pepper to taste and cook for 3–4 minutes or until well browned, then turn and cook on the other side for 2–3 minutes or until browned. Remove the veal from the pan and set aside.

Melt the butter in the pan. Add the onion, celery, carrot and prosciutto and cook over medium heat for 2–3 minutes or until lightly coloured. Return the veal to the pan and cook for another 3 minutes. Add the wine, increase the heat to high and cook for 15 minutes or until it has evaporated. Add the tomato, bring to the boil, then add enough stock to just cover the meat and return to the boil. Cover tightly with the lid or foil, then transfer to the oven to cook for 2½ hours. Uncover and cook for another 20 minutes or until the meat starts to fall off the bones.

Meanwhile, to make the gremolata, combine the parsley, lemon zest and garlic in a bowl.

Place the risotto on plates, top with the veal, spoon over the sauce, sprinkle with the gremolata and serve.

OCA CON LE VERZE

GOOSE WITH SAVOY CABBAGE

I love this dish because the Savoy cabbage absorbs all of the flavours while it cooks with the goose. Savoy cabbage is a typical accompaniment in Lombardian cooking – I also really like it braised with pork ribs. Goose prepared this way is also popular in nearby Piedmont, as well as in the Italian-speaking Swiss canton of Ticino.

Serves 6

2½ tablespoons extra virgin olive oil

50 g unsalted butter

1 white onion, chopped

1 stalk celery, chopped

2 roma (plum) tomatoes, chopped

1 fresh bay leaf

salt flakes

200 ml grapeseed oil

1 × 2.3 kg goose (order from your butcher), brought to room temperature, prepared and cut into 8 pieces (see page 226)

50 ml chardonnay vinegar (see page 226)

1 Savoy cabbage, outer leaves discarded or reserved for another purpose, inner leaves thinly sliced

2 cups (500 ml) Chicken Stock (see page 222)

Place the olive oil and butter in a large ovenproof frying pan over high heat. When the butter melts, add the onion and celery and cook for 5 minutes or until they start to soften. Stir in the tomato, bay leaf and salt to taste, then set aside.

Preheat the oven to 150°C.

Heat the grapeseed oil in a large heavy-based frying pan or wok over high heat, then add the marylands and cook, turning to brown on all sides and carefully ladling the hot oil over the skin, for 6 minutes or until crisp and well coloured all over. Using tongs, add the marylands to the onion mixture, and return the pan to medium heat.

Repeat with the mini-drumsticks, neck, backbone and ribs, frying for 3 minutes or until crisp and well coloured all over. Using tongs, add the goose pieces to the onion mixture, then add the vinegar, cabbage and stock. Cook over medium heat for 12 minutes, stirring occasionally, then cover tightly and transfer to the oven to cook for 2 hours.

Meanwhile, add the breast to the pan or wok of hot oil, skin-side down, and cook, carefully ladling the hot oil over it, for 6 minutes or until crisp and well coloured. Using tongs, remove from the oil, place on a rack over a tray and set aside until cool, then cover and refrigerate until 20 minutes before finishing cooking in the oven.

Remove the frying pan from the oven and set aside in a warm place.

Increase the oven temperature to 250°C. Transfer the breast to the onion and cabbage mixture and roast in the oven for 18 minutes. Remove from the pan, cover, and set aside in a warm place for 5 minutes.

Spread the onion and cabbage mixture on a platter, cut the marylands into drumsticks and thighs and arrange on the cabbage with the neck and mini-drumsticks. Slice the breast meat from the backbone and ribs, discarding the backbone and ribs, then arrange on the platter and serve.

FARAONA AL MASCARPONE

MASCARPONE-FILLED GUINEA FOWL ROASTED IN MILK

Poultry cooked in milk is an ancient dish, though in Lombardy, which is Italy's largest dairy-producing region, we cook a lot of other meats, including beef and pork, in milk too. I took the technique of ladling hot oil over poultry during shallow-frying from the Chinese – it's not something I've seen in Italy, but it gives a wonderfully crisp skin. Guinea fowl can be purchased from good poultry suppliers, and you'll need cotton thread and a needle to sew up the cavity. While I suggest the baked polenta below, you could serve it with any of the polenta recipes on pages 49–55.

Serves 4

1 × 1 kg guinea fowl, wing tips and head discarded, brought to room temperature

250 g mascarpone

fine salt and freshly ground black pepper

75 g unsalted butter

1 small white onion, roughly chopped

1 carrot, roughly chopped

1 stalk celery, roughly chopped

300 ml grapeseed oil

150 ml dry white wine

150 ml milk

Baked Polenta with Tomato Sauce (see page 55), to serve

Rinse out the cavity of the guinea fowl well with cold water to remove any remaining offal or blood, then pat dry. Place the mascarpone inside the cavity and sew up the opening using undyed cotton thread. Sprinkle with salt and pepper and truss with kitchen twine.

Preheat the oven to 200°C.

Melt the butter in a large ovenproof saucepan over medium heat. Add the onion, carrot and celery and cook for 10 minutes or until the onion is lightly coloured.

Meanwhile, heat the oil in a large heavy-based frying pan or wok over high heat. Add the guinea fowl and, trying to keep the cavity opening higher than the rest of the bird so that not too much mascarpone runs out, cook, turning to brown it on all sides and carefully ladling the hot oil over the skin, for 6 minutes or until crisp and well coloured all over. Remove and set aside.

Add the wine and salt to taste to the vegetables, then increase the heat to high and cook for 2–3 minutes or until most of the wine has evaporated. Stir in the milk, then add the guinea fowl, cover tightly with foil and roast for 30–40 minutes or until the juice runs clear when a thigh joint is pierced. Uncover and return to the oven for 5 minutes to colour.

Remove the guinea fowl from the saucepan and set aside.

Press the cooking liquid and vegetables through a mouli (see page 227) into a clean heavy-based saucepan (alternatively, use a stick blender to purée). Place over low heat to keep warm.

Cut the guinea fowl into 8 pieces and arrange on a platter. Pour the sauce over the top and serve with the baked polenta.

154

EPRE IN SALMI

HARE BRAISED IN RED WINE

This is one of my all-time favourite dishes. My *nonno* used to hunt hare in the hills around our village and my *nonna* would marinate them in red wine for several days, until they smelled so strong I thought they were off – I wouldn't recommend that! After we ate this dish, *Nonna* would pick any remaining meat off the bones and make a ragù for pasta. You'll need to start this recipe a day ahead of cooking to give the hare time to marinate. Hare can be ordered online from Vic's Meat (vicsmeat. com.au). Rabbit isn't suitable for this as it needs to be a dark, gamey meat, but you could use venison shoulder or pheasant instead. Here I've served this with white polenta. Keep an eye on timing and start preparing the polenta 20 minutes before the hare is cooked to ensure they are ready to serve at the same time.

Serves 6

1 × 1.2 kg hare, cleaned and cut into 12 pieces

2 litres red wine

2 white onions, diced

2 carrots, diced

2 stalks celery, diced

4 cloves garlic, peeled

6 sprigs thyme, leaves picked

5 juniper berries

5 cloves

2 fresh bay leaves

pinch of freshly grated nutmeg

100 g unsalted butter

100 g lardo (see page 225), chopped

salt flakes and freshly ground black pepper

plain flour, for dusting

100 ml extra virgin olive oil

Soft Polenta (see page 49), to serve

Place the hare, wine, onion, carrot, celery, garlic, thyme, juniper berries, cloves, bay leaves and nutmeg in a glass or ceramic container, then cover and refrigerate for 24 hours.

Remove the hare from the marinade, then strain the marinade, reserving the wine and vegetables separately. Discard the spices and bay leaves. Set aside for 30 minutes to bring to room temperature.

Preheat the oven to 140°C.

Melt the butter in a large heavy-based saucepan over high heat. Add the lardo and reduce the heat to low–medium, then add the reserved vegetables and salt and pepper, and cook, stirring occasionally, while preparing the hare.

Meanwhile, pat the hare dry and dust with flour, shaking off the excess. Heat a heavy-based frying pan over high heat. Add the oil and fry the hare, in batches, for 2 minutes on each side or until coloured, adding each batch to the vegetables as soon as it's ready.

When all the hare is added, cover with the reserved wine and bring to the boil. Cover tightly with foil, then cook in the oven for 2 hours. Increase the oven temperature to 170°C and cook for another 1 hour.

Remove the hare from the liquid and press the liquid and vegetables through a mouli (see page 227) or a fine-mesh sieve over a heavy-based saucepan, pushing down with the back of a ladle to extract as much liquid as possible; discard the solids. Place the saucepan over medium heat and cook for 5–10 minutes or until the liquid has reduced to the consistency of pouring cream. Return the hare to the sauce and stir to coat well.

Arrange the hare on a platter, cover with the sauce (or serve straight from the pan) and serve with polenta.

DAI FORNELLI

FROM THE PAN

My earliest memories are of *Mamma* making polenta in a large copper pot over our open fireplace, which in those days she used for all of her cooking. *Mamma* also cooked with the traditional soapstone pots and pans that have been made in Valtellina for centuries. These pots and pans were ideal for cooking over a fire, giving the same result to slow-cooked food that oven baking gives today – in fact, our word for frying pan, *fornelli*, means 'little oven'. Now I use copper pots and pans for pan-frying and slow-cooking on the stovetop, and share my favourite recipes here. Follow the same tips as for baking, then pat food dry before frying, and use a clean, heavy-based pan preheated over high heat.

ACCALÀ CON POLENTA

MILK-POACHED SALT COD WITH POLENTA

Instead of buying salt cod you could salt your own fish. Place 1 kg of skinless ling fillets in a baking dish, cover with a combination of 800 g fine salt and 60 g caster sugar and cover with plastic film, then refrigerate for 48 hours. Wash the salt and sugar mixture off the fish and soak the fish in cold water for 48 hours, changing the water every six hours or so. The milk-poached fish is traditionally prepared the day before, then reheated over low heat and served with freshly cooked polenta. You'll need to start this dish three days ahead of cooking to give the cod time to soak.

Serves 6

1 kg salt cod (baccalà) fillets

25 g unsalted butter

1½ tablespoons extra virgin olive oil, plus extra for drizzling

1 white onion, thinly sliced

15 anchovy fillets in olive oil, drained

plain flour, for dusting

3 cups (750 ml) milk, as needed to cover

60 g Grana Padano, freshly grated

Soft Polenta (see page 49), to serve

freshly ground black pepper

1 small handful (about ¼ cup) flat-leaf parsley leaves, chopped

Soak the salt cod in cold water for three days, changing the water several times a day. Discard any skin, bone and discoloured flesh.

Place the butter and oil in a deep, heavy-based frying pan over low heat. When the butter has melted, add the onion and cook, covered, stirring occasionally, for 10 minutes or until it is soft but not coloured. Add the anchovies and stir until dissolved.

Pat the cod dry, then dust in flour and place in the pan in a single layer. Add enough milk to just cover the cod, then cook, covered, stirring occasionally to ensure it doesn't stick, for 1 hour or until it falls apart when touched.

Remove the pan from the heat, stir in the Grana and cover, then set aside for at least 10 minutes.

Spoon the polenta into serving bowls, and top with the cod and sauce. Season with pepper, sprinkle with parsley and drizzle with extra oil, then serve.

COTOLETTE DI PESCE PERSICO DEL LAGO D'ISEO

CRUMBED SILVER PERCH FILLETS WITH RADISH, FENNEL AND ORANGE SALAD

If you ever visit Lombardy, you'll find this fresh, summery dish in restaurants all around the lakes. It's great served with a salad of whatever vegetables (or even fruit) are in season. I like radish, fennel and citrus in winter, while even fresh berries, such as blackberries and blueberries, are commonly added at the end of summer. It's important to have the bowls of egg, flour and breadcrumbs lined up before you start crumbing the fish, then gently coat one fillet at a time. The fish stays incredibly moist and juicy inside the crumb coating. So simple, so good!

Serves 4

1½ cups (225 g) plain flour

3 eggs

salt flakes and freshly ground black pepper

300 g fine fresh breadcrumbs (see page 226)

8 × 100 g silver perch fillets, skin-on, pin-boned

200 g unsalted butter

Radish, fennel and orange salad

2 bulbs baby fennel, fronds reserved

1 orange, cut into segments (see page 226), juice reserved

4 red radishes, trimmed, thinly sliced

salt flakes and freshly ground black pepper

extra virgin olive oil, for drizzling

Set up three wide, shallow bowls: one with flour, one with eggs lightly beaten with salt and pepper to taste, and one with the breadcrumbs.

Working with one fish fillet at a time, use one hand to dip it into the flour, then the egg, then using the other hand, lift it out of the egg and coat it in the breadcrumbs. Place on a plate and repeat with the remaining fillets, flour, egg and breadcrumbs; layer them between baking paper if needed to prevent them from sticking.

To make the salad, shave the fennel with a mandoline or very sharp knife. Add to the reserved orange juice. Toss together the radish, fennel and orange segments, season with salt and pepper to taste, then add a drizzle of oil and enough of the orange juice to just coat it all. Add a few fennel fronds. Set aside.

Melt the butter in a heavy-based non-stick frying pan over high heat. Cook the fish, in batches if necessary, for 1½ minutes on each side or until crisp, golden and cooked through.

Drain the fish on paper towel, sprinkle with salt and serve immediately with the salad.

AGONI IN CARPIONE

FRIED MARINATED AUSTRALIAN HERRING

The regions of Veneto and Lombardy not only share a border, they have lots of similar recipes. Like Venetian *in saor*, this dish originated as a way to preserve fish, although these days it's simply enjoyed for its sweet–sour flavour. In Lombardy, we make this with eel, freshwater sardines, or any of the small fish from the lakes. Here, Australian herring (what used to be called tommy ruff) works well because the vinegar complements the oiliness of the fish, but use any small fish you like. While a terracotta container is traditionally used, glass is also good – you just need something that won't react with the vinegar, so avoid metal.

Wipe out the belly cavities of the fish with a clean, damp cloth to remove any remaining blood.

Heat the grapeseed oil in a deep-fryer or large heavy-based saucepan until it registers 180°C on a sugar/deep-fry thermometer (see page 227). Season the flour with salt and pepper to taste and dust the fish lightly, shaking off the excess. Deep-fry the fish for 4–5 minutes or until golden brown all over. Drain on paper towel.

Pack the fish, in a single layer, in a suitable-sized heatproof glass container so that it can be completely covered by the liquid.

Heat the olive oil in a heavy-based saucepan over high heat. Add the onion, carrot, celery, peppercorns, clove and thyme. Reduce the heat to medium and cook for 20 minutes. Add the vinegar and wine and bring to the boil, then boil for 2 minutes. Pour the vegetable mixture over the fish and set aside to cool. When cool, cover and refrigerate at least overnight or for up to 3 days. Remove the peppercorns and clove before serving.

Serve the fish and vegetables cold.

Serves 6 as an entrée

800 g Australian herrings, gilled, gutted and scaled

grapeseed oil, for deep-frying

plain flour, for dusting

fine salt and freshly ground black pepper

50 ml extra virgin olive oil

1 white onion, thinly sliced

1 carrot, finely chopped

1 stalk celery, finely chopped

3 black peppercorns

1 clove

4 sprigs thyme

200 ml chardonnay vinegar (see page 226)

200 ml dry white wine

ANGUILLA ALLA GARDESANA

FRIED EEL WITH TOMATO

Skinning the eel is the hardest part of this recipe – you may need to pre-order them, and a good fishmonger will kill and clean them for you. Traditionally this dish is stored in a terracotta container. It's never eaten on the day it's made as it gets better when it's stored, and can be refrigerated for up to four days.

Serves 4

2 × 600 g eels

¼ cup (60 ml) extra virgin olive oil

1 white onion, finely chopped

1 carrot, finely chopped

¼ cup (60 ml) white wine

250 g drained tinned whole, peeled Italian tomatoes

2 fresh bay leaves

10 basil leaves, torn

salt flakes and freshly ground black pepper

grapeseed oil, for deep-frying

plain flour, for dusting

crusty bread, boiled rice or potatoes, to serve

Place the eels in the freezer for 24 hours, then take them out and leave at room temperature for 30–60 minutes to start to thaw. Pin the eels to a chopping board or clean piece of wood by driving a sharp clean nail, or the tip of a small sharp knife, through their heads. Cut around the necks with a sharp knife and, using a pair of clean pliers, peel the skin back from the necks to the tails. Cut off the heads and discard. Cut an incision along each belly and use a spoon to scrape out the belly cavity. Trim off and discard the back fin. Wash well under cold water. Set aside.

Heat the olive oil in a heavy-based saucepan over medium heat. Add the onion and carrot and cook for 5 minutes or until softened but not coloured. Add the wine and cook for 2–3 minutes or until it has evaporated.

Using a wooden spoon, press the tomatoes through a fine-mesh sieve into the pan, then add the bay leaves and basil and season with salt and pepper to taste. Reduce the heat to low and cook for 25 minutes or until slightly thickened.

Meanwhile, cut the eels through their backbone into 5 cm-thick slices. Wash well and pat dry. Heat the grapeseed oil in a deep-fryer or large heavy-based saucepan until it registers 180°C on a sugar/deep-fry thermometer (see page 227).

Dust the eel lightly with flour, shaking off the excess. Carefully place in the hot oil, in batches if necessary, and deep-fry for 3–4 minutes or until golden brown. Using a slotted spoon, lift the eel out of the oil and place on paper towel to drain.

Sprinkle the eel with salt and pack into a small heavy-based saucepan, pour over the hot sauce and cook over very low heat for 10 minutes. Remove from the heat, set the eel and sauce aside to cool, then cover the pan and refrigerate overnight.

When you're ready to serve, place the pan of eel mixture over low heat until it's simmering. Transfer the eel and sauce to a serving dish and serve with crusty bread, boiled rice or potatoes.

COTOLETTE MILANESE

CRUMBED VEAL CUTLETS MILAN-STYLE

You can see the Germanic influence in this dish from Milan, which is only four hours' drive from Vienna. We call the beaten cutlets *orecchie di elefante* (elephant's ears), because of their shape and size – they should virtually hang over the plate. I pan-fry these in clarified butter as it has a higher burning point than regular butter, but you could use ghee. This is always served with lemon wedges or halves and usually potatoes – either hand-cut chips (as pictured opposite) or roasted with rosemary. If you want to serve some greens alongside, the Silverbeet Cooked in Milk on page 25 would be good.

Serves 6

6 × 350 g veal cutlets, brought to room temperature

plain flour, for dusting

fine salt

4 eggs

300 g fine fresh breadcrumbs (see page 226)

750 g clarified butter (see page 226)

3 lemons, halved

Preheat the oven to 60°C (or the lowest setting your oven has).

Place a cutlet on a sheet of freezer film or baking paper, top with another sheet, then gently beat with a kitchen mallet until it's about 5 mm thick. Repeat with the remaining cutlets.

Set up three wide, shallow bowls: one with flour seasoned with salt, one with eggs lightly beaten with salt, and one with the breadcrumbs.

Working with one cutlet at a time, and holding it by the bone, use one hand to dip it into the flour, then the egg, then using the other hand, lift it out of the egg and coat it in the breadcrumbs. Place on a plate and repeat with the remaining cutlets, flour, egg and breadcrumbs; layer between baking paper if needed to prevent them from sticking.

Using the back of a cook's knife, press along the cutlets at 2 cm intervals, then turn 90 degrees and repeat, creating a cross-hatch pattern; this helps ensure the breadcrumbs stick well to the meat during cooking.

Heat the clarified butter in a wide, deep, heavy-based frying pan until it registers 110°C on a sugar/deep-fry thermometer (see page 227). Fry one cutlet at a time for 2 minutes on each side or until the breadcrumbs are golden and the meat is just cooked through at the bone. Drain on paper towel and keep warm in the oven while cooking the remaining cutlets.

Sprinkle the cutlets with salt and serve with lemon halves.

UCCELLI SCAPPATI

PANCETTA-WRAPPED PORK NECK

In Lombardy, we make a similar dish to this using very small wild birds when they are in season. This is the version we make during the rest of the year when the birds aren't available – using pork neck. The name literally means 'missing birds'. It's also sometimes prepared for small children who find the taste of the gamey birds too bitter.

Serves 4

12 × 60 g, 5 mm-thick pork
 neck slices

12 slices flat pancetta

12 large sage leaves

salt flakes

150 g unsalted butter

Place a slice of pork on a sheet of freezer film or baking paper, top with another sheet and beat gently with a kitchen mallet until it's about 2 mm thick. Repeat with the remaining pork slices.

Lay the pancetta slices on a clean, dry workbench, about 10 cm apart, and place a slice of pork in the middle of each one. Top with a sage leaf, sprinkle with salt and roll the pork neck around the sage, then wrap the pancetta around the pork roll.

Melt the butter in a large heavy-based frying pan over high heat. When foaming, add the pork rolls and pan-fry for 10–15 minutes or until the pancetta is well coloured and the pork is tender.

Place on a platter and serve.

BOLLITO MISTO

This dish is originally from Piedmont, the region to the west of Lombardy, but it's now popular throughout northern Italy. It's a celebratory dish – or at least one to share with a group – as it's typically made with at least three different types of meat and several accompanying sauces. The tongue can be pickled or fresh; I prefer fresh. If you don't have a large enough saucepan to cook both briskets and the tongue at the same time, use two smaller saucepans. Capons (castrated roosters), are traditionally used; they're available from specialist poultry suppliers and butchers, or you could use a good free-range chicken. Order the pigs' trotters and tails from your butcher in advance.

Serves 12

5 cloves

3 white onions, peeled

2 × 300 g cotechino (see page 225)

6 pigs' trotters, halved lengthways

12 pigs' tails

4 stalks celery, roughly chopped

4 fresh bay leaves

4 black peppercorns

salt flakes

1 × 1.5 kg piece beef brisket

1 × 1 kg piece veal brisket

1 × 400 g veal tongue

1 × 1.5 kg capon or free-range chicken

Salsa Verde (see page 222), to serve

Mustard Fruits (see page 223), to serve

Stick the cloves into 1 of the onions and roughly chop the other 2 onions. Set aside.

Wrap each cotechino separately in foil and pierce each one with 10 toothpicks evenly spaced around it. Place the cotechino in a large heavy-based saucepan with the pigs' trotters and pigs' tails, then fill the pan with cold water and bring to the boil. Reduce the heat to low and simmer, covered, for 3 hours, topping up with boiling water if necessary to keep the meat submerged.

Meanwhile, place the clove-studded onion in a large heavy-based saucepan with half of the chopped onion, half of the celery, 2 bay leaves, 2 peppercorns and salt to taste, then bring to the boil. Add the beef brisket and reduce the heat to low, then cover and simmer for 30 minutes. Add the veal brisket and the tongue, then simmer, covered, for another 2 hours, skimming the surface regularly to remove any froth that floats to the surface, and topping up with boiling water if necessary to keep the meat covered.

At the same time as you add the tongue and veal brisket, place the chicken in a third large heavy-based saucepan with the remaining chopped onion, celery, bay leaves and peppercorns, and salt to taste. Cover with cold water and bring to the boil, then reduce the heat to low, cover and simmer for 2 hours, topping up with boiling water if necessary to keep the chicken covered.

When all the meats are cooked, drain them. Peel the tongue, discard the white part from the back of it and cut into 12 slices. Cut the chicken into 12 pieces (see page 226). Slice the veal and beef brisket each into 12 pieces. Peel the cotechino and cut each one into 6 slices.

Arrange all the meat on platters and serve with salsa verde and mustard fruit.

UMIDO DI CERVO

VENISON BRAISED IN RED WINE

I like to dry-age venison myself for ten days, so I always buy it on the bone, but you can ask your butcher to bone-out a dry-aged venison shoulder for you. Ask him to get venison blood for you too, if possible; if not, pigs' blood will do. You'll need to start this recipe a day ahead of cooking to give the meat time to marinate.

Serves 6

4 sprigs rosemary

8 juniper berries

1 star anise

1 stick cinnamon

10 black peppercorns

800 g venison shoulder meat, cut into 3 cm cubes

1 carrot, diced

½ leek, white part halved lengthways, washed well and diced

1 onion, diced

1 stalk celery, diced

1.5 litres red wine

½ cup (125 ml) grapeseed oil

salt flakes

Chicken Stock (see page 222), if needed

150 ml venison (or pigs') blood (order from your butcher)

15 g dark chocolate, grated

60 g cold unsalted butter, cubed

'Polenta' of Potato (see page 54), to serve

Tie up the rosemary, juniper berries, star anise, cinnamon and peppercorns in a piece of muslin. Place in a large heavy-based saucepan with the venison, carrot, leek, onion, celery and wine, then cover and refrigerate for 24 hours.

Separate the venison and the vegetables, reserving the wine and vegetables and discarding the muslin bag. Pat the venison dry.

Heat ¼ cup (60 ml) of the oil in a large heavy-based frying pan over high heat, add the venison and cook for 10 minutes or until the liquid has evaporated and the venison has browned.

Meanwhile, heat the remaining oil in a large deep heavy-based frying pan or flameproof casserole dish. Add the reserved vegetables and salt to taste and cook for 8–10 minutes or until lightly coloured. Add the venison to the vegetables and cook for 2 minutes, then add the reserved wine and bring to the boil; if the wine isn't sufficient to cover the meat, add enough stock to do so. Cover and cook over low heat for 2 hours.

Drain the venison and vegetables, reserving the liquid in a heavy-based saucepan. Set the venison and vegetables aside to keep warm. Bring the liquid to the boil over high heat, then boil for 10–15 minutes or until reduced by half. Remove from the heat, whisk in the blood and chocolate, then the butter; do not reheat the sauce as it may split.

Immediately return the venison and vegetables to the sauce and serve with the 'polenta' of potato.

ALLINA RIPIENA

STUFFED HEN WITH RADICCHIO SALAD

This is the dish that ignited my interest in cooking – my mother's mother used to make it every Sunday for the extended family. One hen for the family – and another one just for me because I loved it so much! So I asked her to teach me to make it, and discovered how much I enjoyed cooking. This is now *Mamma*'s recipe, and every time she comes to visit me in Australia she makes it for me. In Italy, it's always made with an old 'boiler hen' that's reached the end of her useful life for laying eggs. Here I prefer to use a free-range pullet (young hen), although you could use a rooster just as easily, if you can find one. You'll need a needle and undyed cotton thread to sew up the hen's neck. The resulting stock is never wasted – we either serve it as a separate course before the chicken or use it to make risotto.

To make the stuffing, combine the Grana, breadcrumbs and salt to taste in a bowl. Melt the butter in a heavy-based saucepan over medium heat until it starts to sizzle. Add the garlic and parsley, then pour over the breadcrumbs. Stir in the stock and mix well. Taste and add more salt, if you like.

Rinse out the cavity of the chicken well with cold water to remove any offal or blood, then pat dry. Place the stuffing inside the cavity, reserving ½ cup (6 tablespoons), then sew up the opening using undyed cotton thread. Place the reserved stuffing inside the cavity from the neck end, then fold the neck flap over to enclose, sew up with cotton thread and truss with kitchen twine.

Bring the stock to the boil in a large heavy-based saucepan. Add the chicken and reduce the heat to low; if the chicken isn't completely covered with stock, add enough boiling water to just cover. Simmer for 1 hour. Remove from the heat and set the chicken aside in the stock for 15–30 minutes; it will finish cooking in the residual heat of the poaching liquid.

Meanwhile, to prepare the radicchio salad, combine the radicchio, onion and vinegar in a small stainless-steel or glass bowl.

Remove the chicken from the stock, reserving the stock for another use. Cut the chicken into 12 pieces (see page 226) and arrange on a platter. Serve with the radicchio salad.

Serves 6

1 × 1.5 kg chicken

3 litres Chicken Stock
  (see page 222)

Stuffing

80 g Grana Padano, freshly grated

170 g fine fresh breadcrumbs
  (see page 226)

salt flakes

100 g unsalted butter

2 small cloves garlic,
  finely chopped

1 handful (½ cup) flat-leaf parsley
  leaves, chopped

100 ml Chicken Stock (see
  page 222)

Radicchio salad

2 heads radicchio, thinly sliced

1 small red onion, thinly sliced

1 tablespoon cabernet sauvignon
  vinegar (see page 226)

BUSECCA

MILAN-STYLE TRIPE WITH BEANS

You'll need to start this recipe a day ahead to give the beans time to soak. Traditionally it is made with two different types of tripe – honeycomb for flavour and bible for texture (see page 226). If you can get some bible tripe, use half and half, otherwise just use honeycomb. Butchers sell tripe already cooked and bleached (or 'scalded'), ready to be cooked without any further preparation. The finished dish should be quite soupy.

Melt the butter in a heavy-based saucepan over medium–high heat. Add the lardo, onion, carrot, celery stalk and leaves, garlic, parsley, thyme and sage and cook for 8–10 minutes or until lightly coloured. Stir in the tripe and salt and cook for 3 minutes. Add the wine and boil for 12 minutes, then add the stock and return to the boil. Reduce the heat to low and simmer, stirring occasionally, for 30 minutes or until reduced to about one-third.

Drain the beans and add them to the pan along with the tomato. Cook, covered, for another 2½ hours or until the tripe is tender. Remove from the heat, and set aside, covered, for 30 minutes to rest.

Spoon into bowls and sprinkle with Grana. Serve with bread.

Serves 8

50 g unsalted butter

1 × 50 g piece lardo (see page 225), chopped

1 onion, finely chopped

1 carrot, chopped

1 stalk celery, chopped

20 pale celery leaves, finely chopped

1 clove garlic, finely chopped

1 handful (about ½ cup) flat-leaf parsley leaves, finely chopped

3 sprigs thyme, leaves picked

2 sage leaves, finely chopped

1 kg honeycomb tripe (see page 226), cut into 6 cm × 1 cm strips

1 tablespoon salt flakes

200 ml dry white wine

2 cups (500 ml) Chicken Stock (see page 222)

200 g dried borlotti beans, soaked overnight in cold water

450 g tinned whole, peeled Italian tomatoes, chopped

40 g Grana Padano, freshly grated

crusty bread, to serve

ROGNONI TRIFOLATI

KIDNEYS WITH GARLIC AND PARSLEY

This dish is very simple, yet very delicious. The parsley releases all its flavour when it touches the hot butter. You take the pan from the heat and add the lemon juice to stop the cooking (it makes a great *shhhh* sound), then enjoy the kidneys while it's hot!

Serves 4

700 g veal kidneys

1½ tablespoons chardonnay vinegar (see page 226)

20 thin slices ciabatta

2 tablespoons extra virgin olive oil, plus extra for brushing

50 g unsalted butter

1 clove garlic, finely chopped

1 handful (about ½ cup) flat-leaf parsley leaves, chopped

salt flakes

½ lemon

Preheat the oven to 180°C.

Wash the kidneys under cold water, removing all the membrane and fat from the surface. Place in a stainless-steel or glass bowl of cold water with the vinegar to soak for 30 minutes.

Meanwhile, place the ciabatta slices on a baking tray, brush with extra oil and cook in the oven for 6 minutes or until golden. Set aside.

Drain the kidneys, then pat dry and thinly slice the lobes, discarding any visible fat.

Heat a heavy-based frying pan over high heat. Add the oil and, when hot, add the kidney and cook for 2 minutes. Transfer the kidney to a plate, drain the liquid from the pan and return the pan to high heat. Add the butter, garlic, parsley and salt to taste, then cook for 1–2 minutes or until foaming. Return the kidneys to the pan and cook for about 30 seconds.

Remove the pan from the heat, add a squeeze of lemon juice and toss to combine well. Transfer the kidney mixture to a serving plate and serve with the toasted ciabatta.

INGUA IN AGRODOLCE

SWEET AND SOUR TONGUE

I love tongue as a meat; when I was growing up we ate it simply poached with Salsa Verde (see page 222) and mayonnaise, a bit like Bollito Misto (see page 173). As this recipe comes from Lake Como, on the border of Piedmont, it isn't a dish I knew as a child, but when I discovered it, I immediately liked the balance of sweet and acid. It also works very well as an antipasto.

Serves 4

25 g sultanas

1½ cups (375 ml) dry white wine

1 carrot, diced

1 onion, diced

1 stalk celery, diced

1 small handful (about ¼ cup) flat-leaf parsley

1 tablespoon rock salt

1 × 400 g veal tongue

¼ cup (55 g) caster sugar

finely grated zest of 1 lemon

¼ cup (35 g) plain flour

⅓ cup (50 g) pine nuts

2 amaretti, crumbled

salt flakes and freshly ground black pepper

2 tablespoons chardonnay vinegar (see page 226)

mixed leaf salad, to serve

Soak the sultanas in ¾ cup (180 ml) of the wine.

Fill a large heavy-based saucepan with water, then add the carrot, onion, celery, parsley and rock salt. Bring to the boil, add the tongue and return to the boil, then reduce the heat to low. Cover and simmer for 3 hours or until the tongue is tender. Drain the tongue, discarding the liquid and vegetables, and set aside until cool. Peel the skin off the tongue and discard. Cut the meat into 1 cm-thick slices and set aside.

Drain the sultanas, reserving the wine and squeezing them to remove excess wine. Place the sugar and lemon zest in a heavy-based frying pan and cook over low heat until the sugar dissolves. Stir in the flour, sultanas, pine nuts, amaretti and salt and pepper to taste.

Increase the heat to high, add the vinegar and the reserved and remaining wine and bring to the boil. Add the tongue and cook, stirring occasionally, for another 2 minutes or until the tongue is warmed through and coated with the sauce.

Arrange the tongue on a platter, top with the sauce and serve with a green salad on the side.

CONIGLIO ALLA BRIANZOLA

RABBIT WITH MUSHROOMS

In Italy we'd use porcini mushrooms, but slippery jacks or pine mushrooms are great when they're in season in autumn in Australia, or you can use Swiss browns. When frying the rabbit it's important to give it some colour, so don't overcrowd the pan or it will stew rather than fry. If you don't have a large enough pan to cook all of the rabbit in a single layer, cook it in batches. You can serve the rabbit straight from the pan, as I've done here, if you like.

Serves 6

1 × 1 kg rabbit, cleaned and cut into 8–10 pieces

plain flour, for dusting

¼ cup (60 ml) grapeseed oil

200 g unsalted butter

1 white onion, diced

2 carrots, diced

1 stalk celery, diced

5 sage leaves

1 clove garlic, finely chopped

150 ml dry white wine

salt flakes and freshly ground black pepper

200 g tinned whole, peeled Italian tomatoes, chopped

300 g waxy potatoes such as kipfler, peeled and diced

250 g mushrooms, thickly sliced

1 small handful (about ¼ cup) flat-leaf parsley leaves, finely chopped

Wash the rabbit well under cold water and pat dry. Dust lightly with flour, shaking off the excess.

Heat the oil in a heavy-based frying pan over medium heat and cook the rabbit, in batches if necessary, for 5 minutes or until browned all over. Remove the rabbit from the pan and set aside.

Melt 100 g of the butter in the frying pan over medium heat. Add the onion, carrot, celery, sage and half of the garlic and cook for 10 minutes or until the onion is lightly coloured. Add the rabbit, wine and salt and pepper to taste, then boil for 2–3 minutes or until the wine has evaporated.

Add the tomato, then reduce the heat to low and cook, covered, for 20 minutes. Add the potato and cook for another 35 minutes, gently swirling the pan occasionally to ensure the rabbit doesn't stick; do not stir as this will break up the rabbit. Remove from the heat, then cover and set aside to rest.

Meanwhile, melt the remaining butter in another heavy-based frying pan over high heat. Add the remaining garlic, then the mushrooms and cook for 3–4 minutes or until well coloured. Stir in the parsley and salt to taste and remove from the heat.

Arrange the rabbit on a platter with its sauce, pour the mushrooms over the top (or serve in a bowl on the side), and serve.

DOLCI

BAKING
AND
DESSERTS

Like most Lombardians, I love sweets. Many are associated with specific festivals and, when I was young, their appearance added to the anticipation of Carnevale and Christmas. Milan's old city centre is dotted with historic cafés – meeting places for intellectuals, artists and revolutionaries over the years, now they are filled with elegant Milanese who like to see and be seen. Many famous sweets originated in this grand city and are great as desserts or with coffee and a glass of *vin santo* at any time of day.

TORTA SBRISOLONA

CRUMBLY ALMOND CAKE

Sbrisolona means 'crumbly' in my dialect, and when you cut this cake it crumbles due to the ground almonds and polenta. Some people mark lines on the top of the cake when it first comes out of the oven to make it easier to cut once it cools. You can store the cake in an airtight container at room temperature for up to a month. Rendered pork fat (*strutto*) is commonly used in Lombardy, but this is hard to find so you could use extra butter if you prefer. This is delicious served with something creamy, like mascarpone or vanilla gelato, and is typically served to visitors with a glass of white dessert wine.

Serves 8

100 g unsalted butter, diced, at room temperature, plus 25 g extra for buttering

1⅔ cups (250 g) 00 flour (see page 225), sifted

1⅔ cups (200 g) ground almonds

150 g fine polenta

1 cup (220 g) caster sugar

finely grated zest of 1 lemon

2 egg yolks

100 g rendered pork fat, diced, at room temperature

pure icing sugar, for dusting

mascarpone, to serve

Preheat the oven to 180°C. Butter a 20 cm round cake tin with the extra butter.

Place the flour, ground almonds, polenta, caster sugar and lemon zest in a bowl. Add the egg yolks, pork fat and butter and, using your hands, rub into the flour mixture until it just resembles coarse breadcrumbs.

Pour the mixture into the prepared tin and tap it on a workbench to level it.

Bake for 1 hour or until a wooden skewer inserted into the centre of the cake comes out clean. Remove from the oven and set aside in the tin until just warm. Turn out of the tin and dust with icing sugar.

Serve the cake at room temperature with scoops of mascarpone.

TORTA MARGHERITA DELLA ALICE

ALICE'S MERINGUE CAKE

My mum's friend Alice (pronounced Al-ee-chay) is famous for her version of this cake – she sells it to restaurants and at markets all around my valley. The cake used to be cooked overnight, buried in the ashes of the baker's oven after the day's baking was finished. The centre never fully cooks – it becomes like custard and the outside is very light, like a meringue. When you cut it into wedges, the top usually collapses and crumbles and you have the contrast of the two textures – crunchy and creamy. It's traditionally served for breakfast with cappuccino.

Serves 6

unsalted butter, for buttering
90 g potato starch (see page 226), plus extra for dusting
4 eggs
200 g caster sugar
juice of ½ lemon, strained
pure icing sugar, for dusting

Preheat the oven to 180°C. Butter a 20 cm round cake tin and dust it with extra potato starch.

Using an electric mixer, whisk the eggs and caster sugar until thick and glossy. Whisk in the lemon juice. Sift the potato starch into the bowl, a little at a time, folding it in gently after each addition.

Pour the batter into the prepared tin and bake for 25–30 minutes or until the top is golden brown and set like a meringue. Remove from the oven and leave to cool in the tin for 30 minutes.

Turn the cake out onto a plate, then invert onto a wire rack or serving plate. Dust with the icing sugar and set aside to cool.

Dust with more icing sugar, cut into wedges and serve.

190

ANFORTE

In Italian or English, everyone knows what panforte is – literally 'strong bread'. In most regions it contains chocolate, however in Lombardy we make a paler version without it. I didn't like it when I was a kid, but my *nonno* told me it was called panforte because it would make me strong – it worked. I dutifully ate it and now I like it (and I'm strong!). You'll need a sugar thermometer for this recipe.

Serves 20

unsalted butter, for buttering
1 tablespoon honey
440 g blanched almonds, toasted
250 g candied orange, chopped
290 g plain flour, sifted
1 large pinch of ground cinnamon
1 large pinch of ground cloves
1 teaspoon finely grated ginger
½ cup (125 ml) water
400 g caster sugar
pure icing sugar, for dusting

Preheat the oven to 190°C. Butter a 30 cm round cake tin with butter.

Combine the honey, almonds, candied orange, flour, cinnamon, cloves and ginger in a heatproof mixing bowl.

Place the water and sugar in a small heavy-based saucepan over high heat and boil until it registers 110°C on a sugar/deep-fry thermometer (see page 227).

Add the sugar syrup to the almond mixture, mixing quickly to combine well. Pour the mixture into the prepared tin and bake for 20 minutes or until golden brown.

Remove from the oven and set aside to cool in the tin. Turn out of the tin, then dust with icing sugar, cut into wedges and serve with coffee.

Leftovers can be stored in an airtight container for up to 2 weeks.

AMARETTI DI SARONNO
AMARETTI

Makes about 100

3 egg whites (from 55 g eggs)
100 g caster sugar, plus extra
    for dusting
100 g blanched almonds
2 drops pure almond essence
unsalted butter, for buttering

Saronno is a town in the province of Varese, famous for these biscuits and also for an almond flavoured liqueur of the same name. The traditional recipe uses a blend of regular and bitter almonds. As bitter almonds can be hard to find, I've just used regular almonds here and pure almond essence, which is available from some delicatessens and specialist provedores. However, if you can find bitter almonds, use 30 g bitter almonds and 70 g regular almonds and leave out the almond essence. While this recipe makes a lot of biscuits, they are tiny and delicious, and can be stored in an airtight container for ten days or so – but I bet they won't be around that long!

Using an electric mixer, whisk the egg whites with 50 g of the caster sugar until firm peaks form.

Meanwhile, place the remaining sugar in a food processor with the almonds and process until finely ground. Fold the almond mixture and almond essence into the egg white and transfer to a piping bag.

Preheat the oven to 180°C.

Wet two baking trays, line with baking paper, then butter and dust lightly with extra sugar.

Pipe the almond mixture onto the trays into 2 cm discs about 1.5 cm high, leaving a 2 cm space between them, then dust well with more sugar.

Bake for 10 minutes or until the biscuits just start to turn golden.

Turn the oven off and leave the amaretti in the closed oven to cool completely.

NOCCIOLINI
HAZELNUT COOKIES

Makes about 110

unsalted butter, for buttering
4 egg whites
100 g pure icing sugar, sifted
1 pinch of fine salt
100 g hazelnuts, toasted and
    peeled (see page 226)

Hazelnuts feature in many of our sweets as lots of hazelnuts grow in Lombardy near the western border with Piedmont; they're especially abundant in autumn. I like to think that the French took this recipe and 'invented' macarons.

Preheat the oven to 100°C.

Wet two baking trays, line with baking paper, then butter. »

194

Using an electric mixer, whisk the egg whites with the icing sugar and salt until firm peaks form.

Meanwhile, process the hazelnuts in a food processor until finely ground. Fold the hazelnuts into the egg white and transfer to a piping bag.

Pipe ½ teaspoon dots of mixture onto the trays, leaving a 2 cm space between them. Bake for 3 hours or until they are dry enough to lift from the trays without sticking.

Turn the oven off and leave the cookies in the closed oven to cool completely.

Store in an airtight container for up to 10 days.

PANE DEI MORTI
ALL SOULS' DAY BREAD

Makes about 60

250 g amaretti (purchased or see opposite)

60 g sultanas, soaked in warm water for 15 minutes

125 g 00 flour (see page 225), sifted, plus extra for dusting

¼ cup (25 g) cocoa powder

65 g dried figs, sliced

50 g ground almonds

150 g caster sugar

¼ teaspoon ground cinnamon, plus extra to serve

3 egg whites

pure icing sugar, for dusting

Pane dei morti ('bread of the dead'), is served on 2 November, which is known as All Souls' Day. It's typically served with the dessert wine vin santo. Traditionally these loaves are made at least two days before serving and stored in an airtight container so they soften and the inside becomes moist. They'll keep for a week and are delicious toasted, then eaten with cheese. This recipe makes quite a large quantity, as is the Lombardian way, so you could wrap some of the uncooked loaves in plastic film, place them in an airtight bag and freeze them for up to three months, then thaw them before baking.

Preheat the oven to 180°C.

Place the amaretti in a food processor and process to a fine powder. Drain the sultanas and squeeze to remove as much liquid as possible.

Place the flour, cocoa powder, amaretti crumbs, sultanas, fig, ground almonds, caster sugar and cinnamon in the bowl of an electric mixer fitted with a dough hook. Add the egg whites and mix to form a smooth, soft dough.

Tip onto a clean, dry workbench lightly dusted with flour and knead for 1–2 minutes, then shape into six oval loaves.

Place on a lightly floured baking tray and bake for 40 minutes or until a wooden skewer inserted into a loaf comes out clean.

Remove from the oven and place on a wire rack to cool. Slice very thinly, dust with icing sugar and serve with coffee.

Store in an airtight container for up to 10 days.

Pictured from left: Amaretti (page 194); Hazelnut cookies (page 194);
All Souls' Day bread (page 195)

 TORTA DI GRANO SARACENO

BUCKWHEAT CAKE

This cake comes from Valtellina, a picturesque valley in the foothills of the Alps bordering Switzerland. It's too cold for normal wheat to grow there, but buckwheat grows well, and many Valtellina dishes, such as *pizzoccheri* (Buckwheat Pasta with Potato, Cabbage and Cheese, see page 92) *sciatt* (Cheese in Beer and Grappa Batter, see page 26), and this delicious sponge-like cake, use this hardy grain. Toast the walnuts and pine nuts separately in a dry frying pan for a few minutes until they smell aromatic.

Serves 8

100 g unsalted butter, melted, plus extra for buttering

1 cup (150 g) 00 flour (see page 225), plus extra for dusting

⅔ cup (100 g) buckwheat flour (see page 225)

6 eggs

300 g caster sugar

fine salt

50 g walnuts, toasted and finely chopped

50 g hazelnuts, toasted and peeled (see page 226) and finely chopped

50 g pine nuts, toasted and finely chopped

5 g dried yeast

370 g blueberry jam

pure icing sugar, for dusting

whipped cream, to serve

Preheat the oven to 170°C. Butter and flour a 23 cm round cake tin.

Sift the 00 flour and buckwheat flour into a bowl.

Using an electric mixer, whisk the eggs, caster sugar and a pinch of salt until firm peaks form. With the motor running on the lowest speed, sprinkle in the combined 00 and buckwheat flours, then the walnuts, hazelnuts and pine nuts, scraping down the side of the bowl from time to time. Turn off the mixer and fold in the butter, then the yeast.

Pour the batter into the prepared tin and bake for 40–50 minutes or until a wooden skewer inserted into the centre comes out clean. Remove from the oven, set aside to cool a little, then turn out onto a wire rack and set aside to cool completely.

Slice the cake in half widthways. Spread the bottom half with jam and replace the top half.

Dust with icing sugar and serve in slices with whipped cream on the side.

This cake is best eaten on the day of making, but leftovers will keep in an airtight container in a cool place for a few days.

CHARLOTTE ALLA MILANESE

APPLE PIE FROM MILAN

This dish reminds me of British apple pie. Russet apples have the perfect texture for it, plus they don't release too much liquid. If they're unavailable, use another similar apple that's not too juicy, such as gala.

Serves 8

1 kg russet apples

⅓ cup (80 ml) dry white wine

finely grated zest of 1 lemon

180 g caster sugar

1 pinch of fine salt

¼ cup (40 g) sultanas

60 g mixed peel

60 g unsalted butter

18 slices white sandwich bread, crusts removed

1½ tablespoons dark rum

Mascarpone Cream (see page 215), to serve

Preheat the oven to 180°C.

Peel and core the apples and cut each one into 16 thin wedges. Place in a heavy-based saucepan over high heat with the wine, lemon zest and 90 g of the caster sugar. Bring to the boil, then reduce the heat to medium and cook, covered, for 10 minutes. Uncover, add the salt and cook for another 15 minutes or until the liquid has evaporated. Remove from the heat, stir in the sultanas and mixed peel, then cover and set aside.

Beat the butter and remaining sugar with a wooden spoon until well combined. Use three-quarters of this mixture to butter the base and side of a 23 cm round springform cake tin. Completely line the base and side of the tin with the bread, cutting the slices to fit as necessary and reserving some for the top, pressing gently to secure them in place.

Fill with the apple mixture, then top with the remaining bread and spread the remaining butter mixture over the top.

Bake for 40 minutes or until the bread is lightly golden. Remove from the oven, immediately pour the rum over the top and set aside for 30 minutes.

Serve warm with a bowl of mascarpone cream on the side.

BOSSOLÀ BRESCIANO

BRESCIAN-STYLE 'PANETTONE'

This may seem complicated – but it is easy enough if you follow the steps. It's great served with coffee or as a dessert with Zabaglione (see page 204), as pictured opposite. Make sure you use bread flour, and start this recipe the day before to give the dough time to rest overnight.

Serves 8

First dough
⅓ cup (50 g) bread flour, sifted

15 g caster sugar

10 g fresh yeast

50 ml water

Second dough
60 g bread flour, sifted

25 g caster sugar

2 tablespoons water

10 g unsalted butter, melted

Third dough
⅔ cup (100 g) bread flour, sifted

30 g caster sugar

75 ml water

35 g egg yolk (from about
  2 × 60 g eggs)

Fourth dough
1⅓ cups (200 g) bread flour, sifted

50 g caster sugar

35 g egg yolk (from about
  2 × 60 g eggs)

50 g unsalted butter, softened

5 g cocoa butter (see page 225),
  melted

5 g fine salt

Final addition
135 g unsalted butter, at room
  temperature, plus extra for
  buttering

¼ cup (40 g) pure icing sugar,
  sifted, plus extra for dusting

To prepare the first dough, place the flour, caster sugar, yeast and water in the bowl of an electric mixer fitted with a paddle attachment. Mix on low speed for 10 minutes. Cover with a clean, dry cloth and set aside for 35 minutes.

For the second dough, place the flour, caster sugar, water and melted butter in a separate bowl and mix with a wooden spoon until well combined. Add to the mixture in the bowl of the electric mixer and mix with the paddle attachment on low speed for 10 minutes. Cover with a clean, dry cloth and set aside for 40 minutes.

For the third dough, place the flour, caster sugar, water and egg yolk in a clean bowl and mix to form a soft dough. Add to the dough in the bowl of the electric mixer and mix with the paddle attachment on low speed for 10 minutes. Cover with a clean, dry cloth and set aside for 45 minutes.

For the fourth dough, place the flour, caster sugar, egg yolks, butter, cocoa butter and salt in a clean bowl and mix until well combined. Add to the dough in the bowl of the electric mixer and, using the dough hook attachment, mix on low speed for 10 minutes.

For the final addition, using a wooden spoon, cream the butter and icing sugar until pale and creamy. Add to the dough in the bowl of the electric mixer and mix on low speed with the dough hook for 10 minutes.

Press plastic film onto the surface of the dough and refrigerate overnight. Roll into a sausage shape about 40 cm long. Place in a well-buttered 24 cm savarin mould and allow the dough to rise for 8 hours at room temperature (20–24°C) or until it has doubled in size.

Preheat the oven to 160°C.

Bake for 1 hour or until a wooden skewer inserted into the centre comes out clean. Remove from the oven and set aside for 10 minutes, then turn out onto a wire rack and set aside to cool completely. Dust with the icing sugar, cut into wedges and serve.

ABAGLIONE

When I was young, it always amazed me how *Nonna* measured the sugar and wine for zabaglione in a half egg shell. She'd crack the first egg and then measure one half-shell of sugar per egg and one half-shell of wine – it's clever because if the eggs were slightly larger you would also need slightly more sugar and wine. Traditionally the mixture is whisked in a copper bowl – it's worth investing in one as the copper reacts with the eggs during whisking and gives a lighter, fluffier result. If you make the Brescian-style 'Panettone', it is delicious served alongside (see picture on page 203).

Serves 6

5 egg yolks (from 60 g eggs)
100 g caster sugar
finely grated zest of 1 orange
100 ml sweet white wine
biscotti, to serve

Place the egg yolks, sugar, orange zest and wine in a heatproof bowl and whisk to combine. Place over a heavy-based saucepan of simmering water, ensuring that the water doesn't touch the bottom of the bowl, and continue whisking for 8–10 minutes or until the zabaglione is thick and glossy.

Serve in bowls with biscotti on the side.

CHIACCHIERE

DEEP-FRIED CARNEVALE PASTRIES

These pastries are made all over Italy and are traditionally served during Carnevale, the celebration before the fasting of Lent. Commonly called *crostoli*, every region has their own name for them. We call them *chiacchiere*, which means 'chatter', because of the crunchy noise they make when you eat them (though I love how in my mum's dialect they call them *lattughe*, meaning 'lettuce' as they are the shape of lettuce leaves). This is the version *Mamma* makes every year. While a pasta machine makes rolling the dough a lot easier, you could use a rolling pin. It will take a while to deep-fry so many pieces, but they're usually made to feed a crowd. These pastries can be stored in an airtight container for 24 hours – no longer or they'll go soggy. That shouldn't be a problem as they're irresistible!

Makes about 60

275 g 00 flour (see page 225), sifted, plus extra for dusting

50 g caster sugar, plus extra for dusting

2 eggs, lightly beaten

2½ tablespoons dry white wine

1 teaspoon grappa (see page 225)

grapeseed oil, for deep-frying

pure icing sugar, for dusting

Combine the flour and caster sugar on a clean, dry workbench and make a well in the centre. Add the egg, wine and grappa to the well. Using a fork, slowly mix the flour into the egg, then use a plastic pastry scraper and your fingers to bring it all together. Knead on a clean, dry workbench lightly dusted with flour for 2–3 minutes or until smooth. Wrap in plastic film and refrigerate for at least 30 minutes and at most 1 hour; no longer or it will be too firm to roll through the pasta machine.

Cut the dough into six pieces and flatten one piece slightly into a neat rectangle. Wrap the remaining pieces in plastic film to prevent them drying out. Starting on the widest setting of a pasta machine, pass the flattened dough through the machine repeatedly, reducing the setting by two notches each time, until it is 1 mm thick. Dust lightly with flour if it starts to stick; if it becomes too long to handle, cut it in half, dust the half you aren't working with lightly with flour and continue with each half separately. Repeat with the remaining dough.

Place a dough strip on a clean, dry workbench lightly dusted with flour and cut on the diagonal into 5 cm lengths. Make a lengthways cut down the centre of each length, leaving a 1 cm border at both ends uncut. Place on a lightly floured baking tray. Repeat with the remaining strips, stacking the lengths on the tray with a clean tea towel between each layer.

Heat oil for deep-frying in a large heavy-based saucepan or deep-fryer until it registers 180°C on a sugar/deep-fry thermometer (see page 227).

Working in batches of a few pastries at a time, fry for 1–2 minutes, turning once, until golden. Drain on paper towel and, while still warm, dust with caster sugar. When ready to serve, dust with the icing sugar.

RITTELLE DI RISO

RICE FRITTERS

These are another Carnevale treat, traditionally prepared in huge batches. We serve them as a dessert with mascarpone or custard – or just as a snack. This quantity will easily make dessert for six to eight people. You can halve the ingredients if you prefer to make less, and can make the batter the day before and refrigerate it overnight, then add the egg whites just before frying. The easiest way to tell how long to cook them for is to fry a test one first.

Makes about 60

1 cup (200 g) vialone nano rice (see page 59)

1 litre milk

40 g caster sugar, plus extra for dusting

finely grated zest of 2 lemons

fine salt

6 eggs, separated

¼ cup (60 ml) grappa (see page 225)

⅔ cup (100 g) 00 flour (see page 225)

grapeseed oil, for deep-frying

pure icing sugar, for dusting

Place the rice and milk in a heavy-based saucepan over low heat, bring to a simmer, then cook, stirring occasionally, for 10 minutes. Stir in the caster sugar, half the lemon zest and a pinch of salt, and cook, stirring frequently, for another 10 minutes, until the milk has been absorbed and the rice has the consistency of a finished risotto. Transfer to a heatproof bowl and set aside to cool.

Stir in the egg yolks, grappa and remaining lemon zest, then sift in the flour and stir to combine well to form a thin batter. Cover and set aside at room temperature for 10–20 minutes.

Using an electric mixer, whisk the egg whites until firm peaks form. Gently fold into the rice mixture in a few batches.

Heat oil for deep-frying in a large heavy-based saucepan or deep-fryer until it registers 180°C on a sugar/deep-fry thermometer (see page 227).

Working in batches of a few at a time, carefully scoop tablespoons of the rice mixture into the hot oil. Fry, turning the fritters regularly with a slotted spoon, for 5 minutes or until golden outside and cooked inside. Drain on paper towel and dust with extra caster sugar.

Just before serving, dust with icing sugar. Serve warm.

FRITTELLE DI MELA

APPLE DOUGHNUTS

Luckily, *Mamma* also makes these Carnevale sweets every year. They have a great texture because of the pieces of chopped apple through the batter, which also gives them a little acidity. Actually, I think these are my favourite Carnevale treat!

Makes about 36

3 green apples

1⅔ cups (250 g) plain flour

½ teaspoon dried yeast

3 eggs, lightly beaten

1½ tablespoons marsala

1½ tablespoons sparkling mineral water

1½ tablespoons extra virgin olive oil

⅓ cup (75 g) caster sugar, plus extra for rolling

grapeseed oil, for deep-frying

pure icing sugar, for dusting

Peel the apples, cut into 1 mm dice and place in iced water to prevent browning.

Sift the flour into a bowl and, using a wooden spoon, mix in the yeast, egg, marsala, mineral water, olive oil and caster sugar. Cover and set aside for at least 20 minutes. Drain the apple, pat dry and stir through the batter.

Heat oil for deep-frying in a large heavy-based saucepan or deep-fryer until it registers 180°C on a sugar/deep-fry thermometer (see page 227).

Carefully scoop tablespoons of the apple mixture into the hot oil, cooking a few at a time. Fry, turning them regularly with a slotted spoon, for 4 minutes or until golden outside and cooked inside. Drain on paper towel and immediately roll in extra caster sugar.

Just before serving, dust with icing sugar. Serve warm.

Pictured from left: Apple doughnuts (page 207);
Deep-fried Carnevale pastries (page 205); Rice fritters (page 206)

BUDINO DI RICOTTA

RICOTTA PUDDING

If you can, use a patterned savarin mould with a hole in the centre (also called a *budino* mould), as it makes for a very attractive presentation. You could also make this pudding in a baking dish and either turn it out or serve it straight from the dish, if that is easier – it may not look as fancy but will still taste great. This recipe makes a large pudding, but leftovers will keep well, covered and refrigerated, for several days. It's delicious as a snack, with coffee, or even for breakfast. The ingredients can also be halved if you only have a smaller mould or want to make less. The ricotta needs to be quite dry for this dish; if it's very fresh it may make the pudding too wet so wrap it in a piece of clean muslin, then hang it overnight in the refrigerator with a bowl underneath to catch the excess liquid.

Serves 12

100 g sultanas
¼ cup (60 ml) brandy
unsalted butter, for buttering
plain flour, for dusting
10 eggs, separated
¾ cup (165 g) caster sugar
1 kg fresh well-drained ricotta
pinch of fine salt
200 g candied fruit, diced
finely grated zest of 2 lemons
200 g dark chocolate,
  finely chopped

Place the sultanas and brandy in a bowl and leave for 3 hours to soak.

Preheat the oven to 120°C. Butter and flour a 4 litre-capacity savarin mould.

Using an electric mixer, whisk the egg yolks and sugar until thick, pale and fluffy. Add the ricotta and whisk until smooth, then transfer to a large bowl.

Rinse and dry the whisk and the bowl of the electric mixer, then whisk the egg whites and salt until very firm peaks form.

Meanwhile, squeeze the sultanas to remove the excess brandy, discarding the brandy, then gently fold them into the egg yolk mixture with the candied fruit and lemon zest. Fold in the egg white in batches, being careful not to over-mix it.

Pour the mixture into the prepared mould and gently tap it on a workbench to level it. Bake for 1 hour or until the centre is firm to the touch. Remove from the oven and set aside to cool.

Meanwhile, just before serving, melt the chocolate in a small heavy-based saucepan over low heat.

Unmould the pudding onto a serving plate, drizzle with the melted chocolate and serve.

TORRONE DI CREMONA

NOUGAT FROM CREMONA

Cremona is the home of nougat, and they make a hard (*duro*) and a soft (*morbido*) version. High humidity will affect how long it takes the torrone to become hard enough to cut. You could add candied fruit such as orange and cedro, but the sugar from the fruit will result in a softer nougat that won't set enough to cut into neat pieces. You need to start this the day before you wish to serve it, and will need a sugar thermometer.

Makes 8 strips

250 g blanched almonds

200 g hazelnuts, toasted and peeled (see page 226)

140 g honey

500 g caster sugar

100 ml water

3 egg whites

finely grated zest of 2 lemons

6 sheets edible rice paper (see page 225)

Preheat the oven to 180°C.

Spread the almonds on a baking tray and bake for 5–6 minutes or until they turn pale golden. Set the almonds aside.

Place the honey in a small heavy-based saucepan over very low heat and cook for 5 minutes or until it registers 120°C on a sugar/deep-fry thermometer (see page 227).

While the honey is heating, place the sugar and water in another small heavy-based saucepan over low heat and bring to the boil. Boil for 10 minutes or until the syrup registers 160°C on a sugar/deep-fry thermometer.

Meanwhile, using an electric mixer, whisk the egg whites until fluffy. As soon as the honey registers 120°C, with the mixer motor running, slowly drizzle it down the side of the bowl into the egg white, then continue whisking for a few minutes until the mixture doubles in size.

As soon as the sugar syrup registers 160°C on the thermometer, with the mixer motor running, slowly drizzle it down the side of the bowl into the egg white mixture and continue whisking for another 2 minutes. Gently fold in the almonds, hazelnuts and lemon zest.

Line the base of a 40 cm × 20 cm baking tray with the rice paper, slightly overlapping and trimming a sheet if necessary. Pour the mixture on top and spread it out to level the surface. Top with the remaining rice paper and press down with your hands, then top with another tray and weigh it down with heavy tins or a heavy-based saucepan, then leave overnight at room temperature to harden.

Remove the weights and second tray and turn out onto a chopping board. Trim the edges of the nougat and cut into 20 cm × 5 cm strips. Wrap each strip in baking paper, then in foil and store in a cool, dry place for up to 6 months; do not refrigerate.

Break off pieces of nougat and serve with coffee.

LA RUSUMADA
RED WINE ZABAGLIONE

Serves 4

4 egg yolks (from 60 g eggs)

⅓ cup (75 g) caster sugar

50 ml red wine, at
    room temperature

strawberries and savoiardi
    or biscotti, to serve

This dish from Milan is served either for breakfast or afternoon tea. It is usually made with barbera or Barbaresco wine, which are produced in neighbouring Piedmont, but you can use any full-bodied red wine.

Place the egg yolks, sugar and wine in a heatproof bowl and whisk to combine. Place over a heavy-based saucepan of simmering water, ensuring that the water doesn't touch the bottom of the bowl, and continue whisking for 8–10 minutes or until it is thick and glossy.

Serve in bowls with strawberries and savoiardi or biscotti on the side.

SUC
GRAPE CUSTARD

Serves 4

1.2 kg sweet, dark grapes

40 g 00 flour (see page 225)

1 tablespoon caster sugar, or as
    needed to taste

My *nonno* used to make this dessert for me using *primitivo* (zinfandel) grapes. This is a typical dessert served during *vendemmia* (harvest), when there's an abundance of over-ripe grapes needing to be used up – it's just not worth making unless you have deliciously sweet grapes.

Wash the grapes very well in cold water and pick them off the stems. Place in a stainless-steel saucepan and crush lightly with a wooden spoon. Place over medium heat, then cook, covered, stirring and crushing often, for 15–20 minutes or until pulpy.

Strain the grape mixture through a fine-mesh sieve, pressing down to extract as much juice as possible.

Measure 2 cups (500 ml) of the juice, adding a little water if there isn't enough; drink any excess or use it for another purpose.

Place the flour in a mixing bowl, then whisk in a little of the juice to form a paste. Whisk in the remaining juice in 2 batches. Return to the rinsed-out saucepan, taste and, if it's too tart, add a little sugar – how much will depend upon the sweetness of the grapes and your personal taste. Bring to the boil, whisking constantly, then reduce the heat to low and simmer, whisking constantly, for 3 minutes or until thickened. Pour into a heatproof serving bowl and refrigerate for at least 2–3 hours or until set.

Place the bowl in the centre of the table and serve.

CREMA LODIGIANA
MASCARPONE CREAM

Serves 8

4 eggs, separated
2 egg yolks
1 pinch of fine salt
1¼ cups (275 g) caster sugar
400 g mascarpone
¼ cup (60 ml) dark rum
8 Hazelnut Cookies (see page
    194), to serve
mixed berries, to serve

This dish hales from Lodi, a rural area south of Milan, where mascarpone originated. It has the texture of a semi-freddo, and if you set it in the refrigerator for a few hours instead of freezing it, it makes a great accompaniment to cakes such as the crumbly almond cake on page 188 or apple pie on page 200 (see picture on page 201).

Using an electric mixer, whisk the egg whites and salt until stiff peaks form. Transfer to a mixing bowl and set aside.

Rinse and dry the whisk and the bowl of the electric mixer, then whisk the 6 egg yolks with the sugar until thick, pale and fluffy. With the mixer running on low speed, whisk in the mascarpone, then the rum.

Working in batches, gently fold in the egg white mixture.

Divide the mixture among eight ½ cup (125 ml-capacity) ramekins and freeze for at least 3 hours.

Serve with hazelnut cookies and berries.

LA PERSICATA
PEACH JAM

Makes 1 cup (250 ml)

2 kg ripe (about 13)
    white peaches
200 g caster sugar, or as needed

Brescia produces the best peaches in the world. There's a guy in Valle Trompia who has produced peaches for Queen Elizabeth II for the last 30 years. Prince Charles brought him to England to grow peaches there – but the result wasn't the same, no doubt due to the different soil and climate. Sometimes we reduce this jam further to make jellies, like Turkish delight, which we roll in sugar and serve with coffee.

Working in batches, place the peaches in a heavy-based saucepan of boiling water, return to the boil, then remove. Halve and peel the peaches, discard the stones and weigh the peach flesh.

Weigh the caster sugar: for every 100 g peach flesh, you need 10 g sugar. Set the sugar aside.

Process the peach flesh in a blender until smooth. Place in a heavy-based saucepan over medium heat and bring to the boil, stirring often. Stir in the reserved sugar and reduce the heat to medium, then cook, stirring often, for 1½ hours or until very thick.

Store in a sterilised jar (see page 227) in the refrigerator for up to 6 months.

215

BARBAJADA
MILANESE HOT CHOCOLATE

Serves 2

100 g dark chocolate, grated
100 ml pouring (pure) cream
⅓ cup (80 ml) freshly made
    strong espresso coffee, hot

This delicious drink is named after the Neapolitan waiter Domenico Barbaja, who is credited with creating it at the Café Cambiasi, next to Milan's famous La Scala Theatre. The café was a popular meeting place for singers and musicians in the mid-1800s. Originally created as a warming drink to combat Milan's damp, foggy winters, it was very popular until the beginning of WWI, after which it virtually died out. These days Milan's smart cafés are resurrecting it, serving it hot in winter and chilled in summer.

Place the chocolate and cream in a small heavy-based saucepan over low heat and stir until the chocolate has melted. Increase the heat to medium and bring to a simmer.

Pour into 2 cups or glasses, add the coffee and serve.

BARBAJADA SOLIDA
CHOCOLATE COFFEE CUSTARDS

Serves 4

100 g dark chocolate
80 ml (⅓ cup) freshly made
    strong espresso coffee
100 ml pouring (pure) cream
35 g caster sugar
2 egg yolks (from 60 g eggs)
berries, to serve

I love *barbajada* (see above) so much, I created this baked custard dessert using the same simple ingredients. You'll need a sugar/deep-fry thermometer (see page 227) for this dish.

Preheat the oven to 90°C.

Place the chocolate, coffee, cream and sugar in a heavy-based saucepan over low–medium and heat to 40°C on a sugar/deep-fry thermometer (see page 227). Remove from the heat and set aside to come to room temperature. Gently whisk the egg yolks into the chocolate mixture, being careful not to incorporate too much air.

Divide the mixture among four ½ cup (125 ml-capacity) ramekins. Place in a deep baking dish and pour in enough hot water to come one-third of the way up the sides of the ramekins. Bake for 40 minutes or until the custards are just wobbly.

Remove the ramekins from the baking dish and refrigerate, ideally for at least 3 hours or until firmly set (you could make these the day before serving and refrigerate overnight).

Serve with berries on the side.

216

BASICS

FONDO BRUNO
BROWN STOCK

Makes about 2 litres

2 kg veal knuckle, cut into
   3 cm pieces

1 kg chicken bones

50 ml grapeseed oil, plus extra
   for drizzling

2 pigs' trotters, halved

1 large onion, cut into 1 cm dice

1 small carrot, cut into 1 cm dice

1 small leek, white part only
   washed well, cut into 1 cm dice

1 stalk celery, cut into 1 cm dice

75 g trimmed button mushrooms,
   cut into 1 cm dice

100 g tinned whole, peeled Italian
   tomatoes, chopped

400 ml red wine

⅓ cup (80 ml) port

50 g pancetta, chopped

4 litres water

4 black peppercorns

2 juniper berries

4 sprigs rosemary

3 sprigs thyme

1 fresh bay leaf

Ask your butcher to cut the veal knuckle into small pieces as this creates more surface area, which results in a richer flavour. I drive my butcher mad getting him to cut it into 3 cm cubes – see what your butcher can do for you, as the smaller the better. You need to weigh all the vegetables once they are peeled and trimmed to achieve the correct balance of flavour. This reduction is used to add flavour and depth to sauces, braises and risotto, or reduced further to use as a glaze for meat or poultry. You don't need a lot but there's no point in making a smaller quantity, so freeze it in ice cube trays for up to six months and pop out a cube or two as needed.

Preheat the oven to 270°C.

Place the veal knuckle and chicken bones in separate baking dishes, then drizzle with a little extra oil and roast for 30 minutes or until evenly coloured.

Meanwhile, blanch the pig's trotters in a saucepan of boiling water for 1 minute. Drain and set aside.

Heat the oil in a large heavy-based saucepan or stockpot over high heat, then add the onion, carrot, leek, celery and mushrooms. Reduce the heat to low–medium and cook, stirring frequently, for 10 minutes or until soft but not coloured. Add the tomato and cook for another 5 minutes or until most of the liquid has evaporated. Add the red wine and port, reduce the heat to low and simmer for 1 hour or until it becomes a paste.

Add the veal knuckle, chicken bones, trotters, pancetta and the water and bring to the boil over high heat. Reduce the heat to low and simmer for 5 hours, skimming often to remove any froth that floats to the surface.

Ladle the stock through a fine-mesh sieve lined with muslin or a clean damp cloth over a bowl, discarding the solids. Set aside to cool, then refrigerate overnight.

Discard the fat from the top of the stock and return it to the clean pan over medium heat; it may have jellied overnight.

Toast the peppercorns and juniper berries in a small dry frying pan over low heat for a few minutes until aromatic.

When the stock has dissolved, add the peppercorns, juniper berries, rosemary, thyme and bay leaf, then reduce the heat to low and simmer for 30 minutes. Set aside to rest for 30 minutes, then ladle through a fine-mesh sieve lined with muslin or a clean damp cloth over a bowl, discarding the solids. Return to the clean saucepan and bring to the boil. Reduce the heat to low and simmer for 2 hours or until reduced to the consistency of pouring cream. Set aside to cool.

Brown stock will keep, covered, in the refrigerator for up to 3 days or in an airtight container in the freezer for up to 3 months.

BRODO DI MANZO
BEEF STOCK

Makes about 2 litres

3 kg beef neck and tail bones, cut into 2.5 cm lengths

50 ml grapeseed oil

2 large carrots, roughly chopped

2 large onions, roughly chopped

1 stalk celery, roughly chopped

1 clove garlic, roughly chopped

2 sprigs thyme

1 sprig rosemary

1 star anise point

3 litres water

Place the bones in a large heavy-based saucepan or stockpot of cold water and bring to the boil. Drain and rinse the bones and the pan. Set the bones aside.

Heat the oil in the saucepan over medium heat. Add the carrot, onion, celery, garlic, thyme, rosemary and star anise and cook for 12–15 minutes or until the vegetables are soft but not coloured. Add the bones and the water and bring to the boil over high heat. Reduce the heat to low, skim to remove any froth that has floated to the surface, then simmer, partially covered, for 2 hours, skimming occasionally. Set aside to rest for 30 minutes, then ladle through a fine-mesh sieve lined with muslin or a clean damp cloth over a large bowl, discarding the solids. When cool, remove the layer of fat from the top.

Beef stock will keep, covered, in the refrigerator for up to 3 days or in an airtight container in the freezer for up to 3 months.

BRODO DI PESCE
FISH STOCK

Makes about 3 litres

1.25 kg white fish bones and heads

grapeseed oil, for drizzling

1 large stalk celery, chopped

1 large onion, chopped

1 small leek, white part only, washed well and chopped

1 small carrot, roughly chopped

50 g mushrooms, chopped

1 small bulb fennel, chopped

1 small handful (about ¼ cup) flat-leaf parsley stalks

1 fresh bay leaf

4 juniper berries

5 black peppercorns

3.5 litres water

1 tomato, halved

2 large lemons, halved

Preheat the oven to 220°C.

Wash the fish bones and heads very well, removing the eyes, gills and any trace of blood. Place them in a baking dish, drizzle with a little oil and roast for 25 minutes or until well coloured.

Transfer to a large heavy-based saucepan or stockpot with the celery, onion, leek, carrot, mushrooms, fennel, parsley, bay leaf, juniper berries, peppercorns and add the water and bring to the boil over high heat. Add the tomato and lemon, reduce the heat to low and simmer for 40 minutes, skimming occasionally to remove any froth that has floated to the surface. Set aside to rest for 30 minutes, then ladle through a fine-mesh sieve lined with muslin or a clean damp cloth over a large bowl, discarding the solids.

Fish stock will keep, covered, in the refrigerator for up to 3 days or in an airtight container in the freezer for up to 3 months.

221

BRODO DI POLLO
CHICKEN STOCK

Makes about 2.5 litres

1.5 kg chicken carcasses
200 g chicken feet
grapeseed oil, for drizzling
3 litres water
1 onion, roughly chopped
1 carrot, roughly chopped
2 slices leek
1 stalk celery, roughly chopped
1 fresh bay leaf
2 black peppercorns
1 small rasher (slice) bacon

Preheat the oven to 180°C.

Place the carcasses and feet in a roasting tin, then drizzle with a little oil and roast for 20 minutes.

Transfer to a large heavy-based saucepan or stockpot with the water, onion, carrot, leek, celery, bay leaf, peppercorns and bacon and bring to the boil over high heat. Reduce the heat to low, skim to remove any froth that has floated to the surface, then simmer, partially covered, for 1 hour, skimming occasionally. Set aside to rest for 30 minutes, then ladle through a fine-mesh sieve lined with muslin or a clean damp cloth over a large bowl, discarding the solids. When cool, remove the layer of fat from the top.

Chicken stock will keep, covered, in the refrigerator for up to 3 days or in an airtight container in the freezer for up to 3 months.

SALSA VERDE

Makes about 1½ cups (about 400 g)

2 soft white bread rolls, torn into
    small pieces
¼ cup (60 ml) chardonnay
    vinegar (see page 226)
10 salted anchovy fillets, soaked
    in water, drained and patted dry
¼ cup (50 g) salted capers,
    soaked in water, drained and
    patted dry
1 clove garlic, chopped
1 teaspoon salt flakes
3 large handfuls (about 3 cups)
    flat-leaf parsley leaves,
    roughly chopped
200 ml extra virgin olive oil, plus
    extra to cover

This sauce, which is a classic accompaniment for Bollito Misto (see page 173), is also great served with any grilled, roasted or barbecued seafood, poultry or meats. This needs to be made as close to serving as possible, as it loses its vibrant colour after a few hours.

Soak the bread in the vinegar for 10 minutes. Squeeze to remove the excess liquid and place in a food processor with the anchovies, capers, garlic, salt and parsley. Process until combined then, with the motor running, drizzle in the oil and process to form a rough paste.

Transfer to a bowl, cover with a thin layer of olive oil, then refrigerate until needed.

222

MOSTARDA DI FRUTTA MANTOVANA
MUSTARD FRUIT FROM MANTUA

Makes about 1 kg

1 kg quinces
500 g caster sugar
juice of 1 lemon, strained
12 drops mustard essence
   (see page 225)

Fruit preserved in a mustard-flavoured syrup, *mostarda di frutta*, is a speciality of both Cremona and Mantua, and a classic accompaniment to Bollito Misto (see page 173). This version, containing sliced quince, is from Mantua; in Cremona it's more commonly made with whole fruits. Instead of quince you can use this base recipe to preserve many different fruits, including pear, apple, rockmelon and figs – and even chestnuts. You'll need to start this recipe three days ahead to give the fruit time to macerate.

Peel and core the quinces and cut into thick slices. Place in a large heatproof bowl with the sugar and lemon juice and mix to combine well. Cover and refrigerate for 24 hours.

Strain the liquid into a small heavy-based saucepan, bring to the boil, then reduce the heat to low and simmer for 30 minutes or until it reaches 105°C on a sugar/deep-fry thermometer (see page 227). Pour over the quince and mix well, then cover and refrigerate for another 24 hours. Repeat the above process, then refrigerate for another 24 hours.

Place the quince with the liquid in a wide heavy-based frying pan over low heat and bring to the simmer, then simmer for 45 minutes or until it registers 105°C. Remove from the heat and set aside to cool to room temperature. Stir in the mustard essence, pack into sterilised jars (see page 227) and store in a cool, dark place for up to 1 year. Once opened, store in the refrigerator for up to 2 months.

BURRO ACIDO
ACID BUTTER

Makes about 500 g

2 cups (500 ml) chardonnay vinegar (see page 226)

1 cup (250 ml) dry white wine

1 golden shallot, thinly sliced

¼ fresh bay leaf

2 black peppercorns

500 g unsalted butter, softened

When you make risotto, you traditionally cook golden shallot or onion in butter before you add the rice, but often it burns a little which changes the flavours. So I use this acid butter (that I learnt from Gualtiero Marchesi), which keeps the flavour of the onion without actually having pieces of onion in the risotto. I use it at the end when we *mantechiamo* (see page 59) the risotto, so it doesn't change the flavour but gives the necessary acidity to cut through the richness of the risotto itself. If you use acid butter, you don't need to add any wine to the risotto.

It is important to reduce the liquid over low heat – don't be tempted to boil it to reduce it quickly or it will have a slightly burnt flavour. It's hard to make this butter in a smaller quantity, but it freezes well, then you have it on hand whenever you make risotto. You can also use it to finish pasta, mashed potato or even to pan-fry seafood – it adds a nice acid/sweetness balance. If you don't want to make the acid butter, start your risotto by frying half a chopped white onion in a knob of butter for 5–10 minutes until it's soft but not coloured, add the rice and toast, then add ¼ cup (60 ml) warm white wine and cook for few minutes before starting to add the stock.

Place the vinegar, wine, shallot, bay leaf and peppercorns in a small heavy-based saucepan. Bring to the boil, then reduce the heat to low–medium and simmer for 30–50 minutes or until reduced to about 1 tablespoon. Press through a fine-mesh sieve and set aside. Discard the solids.

Place the butter in a blender and, with the motor running, add the reduction and blend until well combined and smooth. Transfer to a container (or spread into a log on a sheet of baking paper and roll up tightly) then refrigerate until firm.

Acid butter will keep for up to 2 weeks in the refrigerator and 3 months in the freezer.

GLOSSARY

INGREDIENTS

BAY LEAVES
Always use fresh bay leaves if possible as they have a better aroma. Bay trees are very easy to grow in a pot or garden, they look good and will give you fresh leaves all year round.

BRESAOLA
Air-dried beef popular in Lombardy, it is often aged in the same caves as the region's aged cheeses because mountain air flowing through the caves maintains a cool temperature year-round.

BUCKWHEAT FLOUR
Made from finely milled buckwheat, it has a similar texture to wheat flour but a darker colour and doesn't contain gluten. This is a seasonal product, available from April to September online: lario.com.au.

BUCKWHEAT POLENTA
Made from ground buckwheat, with a similar texture to corn polenta, but a darker colour. This is a seasonal product, available from April to September online: lario.com.au.

CARNAROLI RICE
I use Acquerello brand carnaroli rice aged for one year for my risotto. It's available online from lario.com.au and in some good delicatessens.

CHESTNUT FLOUR
Made from dried ground chestnuts, with a similar appearance to wheat flour, but with a nutty, slightly sweet flavour. Available from some delicatessens and online from lario.com.au.

COCOA BUTTER
This edible vegetable fat is extracted from cocoa beans and used to make chocolate. Available from health food stores.

COTECHINO
Cured Italian pork sausage available from some butchers and delicatessens.

EDIBLE RICE PAPER
Also called edible wafer paper, it is available from the baking section of speciality food stores and some delicatessens, and online: essentialingredient.com.au. It is not the same as the rice paper found in Asian grocery stores, used for making fresh spring rolls.

FLOUR – 00
Also called tipo 00 (or doppio zero) flour, it is a very finely milled Italian flour available from supermarkets, some delicatessens and online at lario.com.au.

FRENCH TARRAGON
This herb is only available during summer, so if you can't get it, use fresh oregano or marjoram, not the similar-looking, but tasteless Russian tarragon.

GRANA PADANO
Grana and parmesan are generic names for hard grating Italian cheeses. In Lombardy we make Grana Padano (a Protected Designation of Origin product), which is similar to the famous Parmigiano Reggiano from the adjoining region of Emilia Romagna – you could substitute that if it's what you have on hand. Most importantly, always buy a whole piece of Grana and grate it yourself – avoid the pre-grated stuff you can buy in supermarkets.

GRAPPA
An Italian spirit distilled from grape skins and seeds left over from wine making available from liquor retailers.

ITALIAN PORK SAUSAGE MEAT
I use the meat from plain Italian-style pork sausages – the pork is coarsely minced, without any herbs or spices added.

LARDO
Pork back fat cured with herbs and spices, it is available from some delicatessens.

MUSTARD ESSENCE
Available online from ingredientbox.com.au. Alternatively, substitute with mustard oil from Indian or Pakistani grocers – experiment with quantity as the strength varies between brands, so add a drop, then taste to see if you need to add more.

MUSTARD FRUITS
Fruit preserved in mustard-flavoured syrup such as chestnuts and apple. Available from specialist provedores.

NETTLES

Available from some greengrocers when they are in season in spring. To prepare, wear thick rubber gloves to prevent stinging (the itchiness can last for days), and pick over and discard the coarse, tough base of the leaves. Cooking removes the stinging element. If unavailable, use spinach, silverbeet or another leafy green.

POTATO STARCH

Made from dried ground potato, it is very soft and fine, and gluten-free. Available from some supermarkets, health food stores and specialist provedores.

PROSCIUTTO

Good-quality prosciutto should be aged for at least 18 months, such as Prosciutto di Parma or San Danielle from Italy or an Australian prosciutto made from Kurobata pork. Buy prosciutto sliced from the leg from a delicatessen.

RICOTTA

Buy fresh ricotta from a delicatessen or specialist provedore, not pre-packed from a supermarket. Very fresh ricotta can be too wet for some dishes, so it needs to be well drained. Hang it wrapped in muslin or a clean cloth overnight in the refrigerator with a bowl underneath to catch the excess liquid.

ROCK SALT

I use rock salt in the water whenever I'm boiling pasta or vegetables as it's inexpensive and always on hand in my kitchen; you could use an inexpensive fine salt if you prefer.

TRIPE

There are three main types of tripe, which is usually the stomach of beef or veal, although lamb, goat or pork stomach can be used. Honeycomb or pocket tripe is the meatiest and most tender, and therefore most commonly used. Less common are smooth, or flat, tripe and bible, or leaf, tripe, which has many thin folds or 'leaves' on the surface.

VINEGAR – CABERNET SAUVIGNON AND CHARDONNAY

Speciality vinegars made from specific grape varieties generally have a softer, less aggressive flavour than general red and white wine vinegars. Forum is a good brand imported from Spain, while LiráH (lirah.com.au) is a similar Australian brand: both are available from selected delicatessens and specialist provedores or online.

METHODS

BREADCRUMBS – MAKING FINE FRESH BREADCRUMBS

This is a great way to use up any stale bread: process stale bread in a food processor until finely crumbed. Freeze in an airtight container or bag for up to 12 months so they're on hand whenever you need them.

BUTTER – CLARIFYING

Melt butter in a saucepan over low heat until the clear yellow fat floats to the top and the white milk solids sink to the bottom of the pan, then carefully pour or ladle the clear fat off, leaving the milk solids behind. Alternatively, use ghee which is a very similar product.

CITRUS – SEGMENTING

Using a sharp knife, cut the top and bottom off the citrus fruit to reveal the flesh, stand it upright and cut down the sides to remove all skin and white pith. Holding the peeled fruit in your hand over a bowl, cut down either side of each of the membranes to remove the segments. Drop all the segments into the bowl and squeeze the remaining membrane over the bowl to collect the juice.

HAZELNUTS – TOASTING AND PEELING

Spread hazelnuts on a baking tray and place in a preheated 180°C oven for 10 minutes or until skins darken, then place in a clean tea towel and rub vigorously to remove most of the skins.

POULTRY – PREPARING AND SECTIONING

To remove any feathers or quills left in poultry, quickly heat the skin with a kitchen blowtorch – this burns off the small ones and chars the others so that they are easy to see and remove with fish tweezers.

Rinse out the cavity well with cold water to remove any remaining offal or blood, then pat dry with paper towel.

Cut off and discard the first two joints (wing tips and wings) of the wings (or reserve for stock). Using poultry shears, cut the bird in half so that both drumsticks and thighs (marylands) are in one piece and both breasts are in a single piece. Cut off the neck and surrounding skin. Remove the wing joints (mini-drumsticks) from the breasts. Cut out the backbone, then the ribs. You should now have 8 pieces: 1 double breast, 1 double maryland, 2 mini-drumsticks, 2 rib sections, 1 neck and 1 backbone. To serve, cut the marylands into thighs and drumsticks and halve, quarter or slice the breast, depending on the recipe.

POULTRY – TRUSSING

Place the bird on a workbench breast-side up with the legs facing you. Place the middle of a metre-long piece of kitchen twine underneath the tail of the bird. Lift each end of the twine up and over the end of the drumsticks, crossing it over them. Pull it tight to draw the drumsticks in together across the entrance to the cavity. Pull the ends of the twine away from you and cross them around the front of the bird over the wings to hold them in place. Carefully turn the bird over towards you so that the neck is now facing you, keeping the twine tight, then tie a knot under the neck to secure. Cut off any excess twine, turn the bird onto its back again and you're good to go.

YABBIES – PREPARING

The most humane (and easiest) method to kill any crustacean is to chill it in the freezer for 30–60 minutes until it becomes insensible (but not long enough to freeze it), then kill it promptly by splitting it in half or dropping it into a saucepan of rapidly boiling water. (See rspca.org.au for more details.) I put the yabbies into a bowl and wrap the bowl in a towel so they don't climb out and walk all over the freezer.

EQUIPMENT

DRUM SIEVE

A cylindrical sieve shaped like a drum used for pushing foods through such as cooked fruit or vegetables to create a purée or sifting dry ingredients like flour. Available from kitchenware stores.

JARS – STERILISING

Line the base of a large stockpot with a clean tea towel, then place the jars in, standing upright, and cover with cold water. Bring to the boil, then simmer for 10 minutes. Turn off the heat, add the lids to the pan, cover and leave to stand for 10 minutes. Using tongs, remove the jars and lids from the pan and drain on a clean tea towel. Fill while the jars are still warm, then seal immediately.

MICROPLANE

Use a microplane for grating citrus zest as it gives a very fine result. They're also good for ginger, cheese, nutmeg – anything you want very finely grated.

MOULI

Italians use moulis for all sorts of vegetable sauces and purées. They were around long before food processors and often give a better result because they create a thick purée, yet filter out the most fibrous parts like the skin and seeds. A stick blender is the best alternative.

POTATO RICER

A potato ricer (which looks like a giant garlic crusher) is an inexpensive investment that gives the best results for mashing potato for gnocchi. You don't have to peel the potatoes, just push them through the ricer while they're still too hot to handle. You could pass them through a mouli (see above) or a fine-mesh sieve, but a ricer gives the lightest texture.

PROBE THERMOMETER

A digital thermometer used to measure the temperature of cooked food, especially meat and poultry. Available from kitchenware stores.

ROTISSERIE FORKS

Used to put onto either end of a spit to hold the meat in place, but you can also improvise with a thick slice of potato on either end. Available from barbecue and hardware stores.

SUGAR/DEEP-FRY THERMOMETER

A number of recipes require precise temperatures, especially sugar syrups in desserts, so invest in a sugar/deep-fry thermometer, available from kitchenware stores. These can also be used to measure the temperature of oil when deep-frying to ensure crisp results.

Roberta Muir and Alessandro Pavoni

ACKNOWLEDGEMENTS

I had no idea how many people it takes to write a cookbook before I started this one. There are so many people to thank:

Alex Keene – thank you for the endless recipe development and testing over months and months. Who needs a day off? You are a hard-working, dedicated, passionate and talented chef, and I am so proud to have now opened our restaurant, Via Alta, together.

Alex Joslyn – the go-to chef for our photo shoot – your prior planning and execution over the shoot days was indispensable, especially as we were waiting every day of the shoot for Jada to be born!

Mamma and *Papà* – thank you for always giving me the freedom to make my own choices and travel the world cooking and living, and for making me the person I am today. Thank you also for helping with the recipe testing when you were here in Australia and for giving us your expertise to get the authentic Lombardian taste as it should be for each and every recipe.

Nonna Maria – the most influential person in my life with regards to food – you gave me the passion and love for food and good produce, and were my first teacher. Without you I wouldn't be a chef today. I only wish you were still here to see all of this.

Elsa and Tulio Freddi – thanks for showing me the food of your mountain, the people, the produce, the hunting and the foraging. And for cooking for us!

Franz and Robbie – thanks for hosting us during the time it took to test all the recipes over and over again. And a special thanks to Franz, not only for his wonderful location photography, but also for opening his special cellar.

Giovanni Pilu – thanks for pushing me to do this book and for being my best friend and supporter.

To Victor Moya (our Ormeggio head chef, business partner and great friend) and the rest of the Ormeggio team – thanks for keeping it all together in my absence while I was working on this book.

To Roberta, my amazing co-author – your attention to detail, consistency, hard work and enthusiasm for this project were inspiring. You never tired of ensuring every line was perfect. A pinch of salt will never mean the same thing to me again!

To my publisher, Julie Gibbs – I am honoured to be part of your 'stable' of writers – big thanks to you and your team. Special thanks to the very talented photographer Chris Chen and stylist Geraldine Muñoz and stylist's assistants, Katie Randell and Danielle Gard. Thanks also to Senior Designer, Emily O'Neill, Designer Alissa Dinallo and Photo Shoot Producer, Cass Stokes, for making our manuscript into such a beautiful book. Big thanks also to Senior Editor Kathleen Gandy for her eagle eye, and Publishing Manager, Katrina O'Brien, for ensuring everything went smoothly and stayed on track.

INDEX

Thank you to the following stockists for providing props for our photo shoot.

Chinaclay: ceramicists Anthony Brink, Ursula Burgoyne, Szilvia György, Marian Howell,
Cath O'Gorman, Timna Taylor, Natalie Velthuyzen and Kati Watson
Little White Dish
Malcolm Greenwood
Sandy Lockwood
Simon Reece
Slab and Slub
Studio Enti
the fortynine

LANTERN

UK | USA | Canada | Ireland | Australia
India | New Zealand | South Africa | China

Penguin Books is part of the Penguin Random House group of companies
whose addresses can be found at global.penguinrandomhouse.com

Penguin
Random House
Australia

First published by Penguin Group (Australia), 2015

1 3 5 7 9 10 8 6 4 2

Design by Emily O'Neill © Penguin Group (Australia)
Photography by Chris Chen, except location photography
on endpapers and pages ii, iii, 115 and 127 by Franz Scheurer
Styling by Geraldine Muñoz
Typeset in 10/14 ITC Century Light by Post Pre-press Group, Brisbane, Queensland
Colour separation by Splitting Image Colour Studio, Clayton, Victoria
Printed and bound in China by C&C Offset Printing Co Ltd

National Library of Australia Cataloguing-in-Publication entry
Creator: Pavoni, Alessandro, author
A Lombardian cookbook: from the Alps to the lakes of Northern Italy /
Alessandro Pavoni, Roberta Muir; photographer Chris Chen.
ISBN: 9781921383380 (hardback)
Subjects: Cooking, Italian.
Other Creators/Contributors:
Muir, Roberta, 1962- author.
Chen, Chris, photographer.
641.5945

penguin.com.au/lantern